Landscape Design Guide

Volume 2
Hard Landscape
The Design of Paved Spaces
Landscape Enclosure
and Landscape Furniture

Landscape Design Guide

Volume 2
Hard Landscape
The Design of Paved Spaces
Landscape Enclosure
and Landscape Furniture

Authors: Adrian Lisney and Ken Fieldhouse

Editor Jeremy Dodd

Gower Technical

Published by
Gower Publishing Company Limited
Gower House
Croft Road
Aldershot
Hants GU11 3HR
England

Gower Publishing Company
Old Post Road
Brookfield
Vermont 05036
USA

British Library Cataloguing in Publication Data
Lisney, Adrian
  Landscape design.
  Vol. 2: Hard landscape: the design of paved spaces,
  landscape enclosure and landscape furniture
  1. Landscape design
  I. Title II. Fieldhouse, Ken III. Dodd, Jeremy
  712

ISBN 0 566 09019 8

Printed in Great Britain by BPCC Wheatons Ltd, Exeter

Contents

Preface

The Department of the Environment has, over the years, produced a number of landscape design guides and landscape brochures. The first was issued in 1971 and the most recent in 1988 as 'Landscape Design for the Nation'. Some, like the Housing Development Notes 'Landscape of New Housing', dealt with the broader concepts of landscape design. Others gave advice on specific landscape topics such as 'Existing Trees and Buildings' in response to the widespread desire to develop land while retaining existing trees with their many and diverse benefits to site quality.

Some years ago it was decided to bring the design guide material together in a more convenient form for the general public as well as environmental design professions and, at the same time, to update it thoroughly. It is now published in two companion volumes in which design with plants is covered by Volume 1: *Soft Landscape* and built works in the landscape covered in Volume 2: *Hard Landscape*.

The design guide firmly concentrates on principles and broad concepts, rather than going into great depth on highly specific aspects of construction or planting because there is such a broad wealth of published material available on every conceivable specialist topic. The essential facts needed to achieve good landscape design are stressed; however, to help those who want to study a single aspect of landscape design in great depth, advice on further reading is given both in the text and more broadly in the bibliography at the end of each volume.

The growing public awareness of the importance of the landscape environment is now apparent in many ways. Public concern extends beyond preserving fine individual trees to conserving the most valuable landscapes on a local as well as a national scale. They are often scenically and scientifically irreplaceable. Beyond that, it extends to development of underused land with ecological and social or recreational potential.

Bleak city areas of ill-considered urban design rebuilt in the 1950s and 60s with inadequate urban landscape provision need to be tackled. Many parks too are no longer attractive because of their open and bleak windswept character. To remedy these conditions, it is necessary to follow a more functionally inspired approach through the art and science of landscape planning, in addition to planting attractive trees and shrubs. For example, shelter planting designed to save energy, to reduce noise and to reduce air pollution can, when used coherently on a city scale, improve living and working conditions. The success of these measures can be observed in towns and cities that once again attract people.

PSA's consultant authors, Adrian Lisney and Ken Fieldhouse, Landscape Architects, in association with the general editor Jeremy Dodd, have been responsible for the text, many sketches and excellent photography. Studies by several landscape consultants including work by Maurice Pickering and the late Clifford Tandy have been incorporated. Additional photography by PSA Photographers and by Tim Jemison.

MICHAEL ELLISON

Chief Landscape Architect

Property Services Agency

February 1990

Acknowledgements

Adrian Lisney and Ken Fieldhouse gratefully acknowledge the particular assistance of Mr M.J. White–The British Aggregate Construction Materials Industries; Mr G. Perkin formerly Cement and Concrete Association; Mr C.J. Powell–The Brick Development Association; Dr A. Dowson–Marshalls Mono Ltd., Concrete paving slabs and concrete block paviors; Dr C. Gill–Timber Research and Development Association; and more generally Rosalyn Guard and Michael Oldham.

We would like to thank the many individual photographers and Michael Oldham for all the sketches and diagrams. We would also like to acknowledge Christine Smith's help in writing the bibliography and Sarah Oram's unstinting efforts in typing the numerous manuscripts.

CHAPTER 1

Introduction

This volume appraises the principles of design and detailing in hard landscape, enclosure and landscape furniture. It also gives practical advice on the selection of materials and products and gives general guidance on construction techniques. However, it does not set out to be a definitive statement on construction techniques, which are adequately described in many specialist publications. Nor is the Guide exclusive in the materials or products it discusses.

Fundamental to hard landscape design is the selection of products and materials, appropriate to their function and sympathetic to their surroundings. For instance, the use of indigenous and traditional materials in rehabilitation projects in towns and cities can be of particular importance where direct relationships with existing fine architecture, street scenes or spaces are to be maintained. Conversely, in a greenfield development site, or in association with an outstanding example of modern architecture, the selection of more modern components and construction techniques may be more fitting. The particular needs of the site and the client's brief need to be investigated in each case.

In all design projects, continuity of materials, components and detailing is important in order to achieve visual unity and harmony. Ill-considered use of materials and lack of continuity in detailing tends to produce a disparate type of landscape architecture that brings few pleasures to anyone.

Hard landscape design is essentially concerned with the design of spaces for people, the main function of which may appear to be pedestrian movement. Generally, however, other functions, which may include active or passive recreation or a place to sit and eat or take in a view, although transient, are key factors in creative design.

Hard landscape often occupies the space between buildings. It provides, at the very least, paved surfaces within these spaces, as well as a general landscape setting for the architecture, but can make a very positive contribution to urban design in the process. It is important, therefore, that hard landscape design primarily relates in its expression, patterning, levels and visual qualities to human scale and movement. Nevertheless, it must also often relate directly to the adjacent architecture. The link between these two functions is generally provided by the vertical elements in the design – the walls, the lighting and, above all, the vegetation, especially the trees.

The use of tall trees in spaces such as these is particularly important. The bottom of the canopy helps to define an upper limit to the view because

Figure 1.2 *Opposite:* Repaving of The Strand in London, 1851. The foreman beats time for the ramming of paving blocks.

movement and activity generally occur below it, while the canopy itself softens and screens buildings beyond. Thus, the space created under the canopy relates directly to the human scale while the overall stature of the trees relates to the surrounding space and buildings.

In some spaces, vehicular movement may be particularly important and so the hard landscape must be designed to perform its function and still be appreciated at speeds faster than the pace of walking.

In both vehicular and pedestrian spaces, the importance of movement and changing views, as perceived by the users, are key features, although frequently underestimated design requirements. Ease of movement, obvious routes, visually interesting journeys with transient views, anticipation and enjoyment are all qualities to be sought.

All forms of constructed landscape have to be designed with ease of maintenance in mind. This in turn demands detailed consideration in the choice of materials and methods of construction. Carefully thought through, these factors can help to make landscape management more effective.

PART 1

Paving Design

CHAPTER 2

Paving Design

Paving forms a significant part of most environmental and building designs. Each site is unique and the design of paved surfaces should emerge from a clear understanding of the possibilities as well as the problems.

Choosing paving materials is a challenging design opportunity. The main factors which affect the choice of particular materials are: appearance, strength, durability, slip resistance, availability, ease of removal for access to underground services, capital and maintenance costs.

This chapter assesses principal materials and methods of construction in order to illustrate the wide range of opportunities, and also examines the general considerations affecting paving design. The characteristics of individual materials are then dealt with in the six that follow.

Some materials, particularly those designed for sporting activities, fall outside the scope of this Guide. These include, for example, semi-porous athletics tracks, artificial turf football surfaces for all-weather play, no-fines concrete tennis courts and smooth concrete roller-skating rinks.

Visual Aspects of the Design of Paved Spaces

Affinity of materials with their location

All landscape materials, including paving, should be selected to suit the individual site. Where the existing landscape character is pleasing, the proposed design is best developed to harmonize with it, so that it may eventually become part of the local scene. An investigation of local materials, new or perhaps reclaimed, and the availability of specific skills required to use them, makes a good starting-point for any landscape design.

The designer's actions can influence the visual character of a whole area. For example, slates, granites or flint used away from their natural source usually seem out of place and are certainly more expensive, because of high transport costs.

Imitation stone is available as an alternative to natural stone. However, its appearance lacks the quality and subtlety of the natural material and, although suitable for certain locations, the two materials do not generally mix satisfactorily.

Pattern and scale

Apart from poured and levelled *in situ* materials, such as plain concrete or tarmac, paving is generally made up of repetitive units. Their size depends on

Figure 2.1   Paving has many varied functions and is an essential element of the way we use and experience our surroundings as with a) a residential footpath, b) sports pitch, c) playground, d) parade ground.

the strength of the material, their function, manufacturing techniques and traditional forms, which are generally related to the ease of laying. Paving patterns can be used to create harmonious or dramatic effects. However, the patterns should be sympathetic to the properties of the materials used and have a positive relationship to the surroundings.

Formal paving, with a well-defined edge and a clear, regular pattern, can be a very bold element in the landscape and, if it reflects the scale of the surroundings, can contribute a sense of calmness to the urban scene. Paving designed with a dynamic pattern reflects a sense of potential activity, which can be stimulating in a major public space, but might be dominant in a smaller area.

For surfacing large areas, such as urban squares, an appropriately large-scale design can be created from small paving units by creating a framework of one material, like brick or granite setts, infilled with another such as precast concrete units or brick of a contrasting colour. Textured surfaces can also be used in the same way – for example, grooved *in situ* concrete panels laid alternately at right angles to each other, or smooth granite panels in a 'framework' of long, coarse, sawn slabs.

Informal patterns harmonize with leisurely movement along uncrowded pathways and paved spaces where there is little emphasis on direct routes. Ground cover or shrubs allowed to grow over the edge, soften and extend the feeling of informality. On the other hand, directional patterns can be used to suggest purposeful movement along a route or, combined with varied widths, to indicate path hierarchies.

Patterns can be used to create optical illusions. Distance can be foreshortened by increasing path width, by varying module size and by accentuating the cross-joints. Conversely, apparent distance can be increased by stressing the longitudinal joints and using a small module which recedes into the distance towards the limit of vision. The same techniques are applicable in enclosed spaces. Small-pattern paving serves to emphasize the sheer size of surrounding buildings, whilst large unit paving can help to reduce the visual scale.

Regularly spaced trees, appropriate to the nature of the place set into paving, by creating a three-dimensional pattern, help to harmonize with the diverse scales of surrounding buildings – for example, in major city squares.

The textural quality of paving is highly significant. It can suggest certain functions, or harmonize with the surrounding landscape or with adjoining buildings. The richness or roughness of the surface, or its high light reflection, can be stimulating. Texture is best appreciated at relatively close quarters. In fact, the quality of finer finishes may be lost in large spaces, unless there are smaller-scale spaces within them.

Contrast in paving materials

Contrast can be achieved through scale, colour, module, texture and by the direction in which units are laid. A mixture of materials or patterns only

Figure 2.2 A relaxing ambience can be created by using informal paving patterns and allowing planting to grow over the edges.

Figure 2.3 Banding in paving will increase or decrease the visual perspective – contributing to the control and structure of space.

Figure 2.4 Even in the use of the same material – here brick – the function can be stressed through bonding direction and scale.

confuses the user about the meaning of the design, whereas consistency in choice of materials helps to make the basic character of a path or paved area more easily understood. Contrasting paving can be used to delineate special functions, such as the high load-bearing capability in a particular paved zone, the degree of privacy expected by residents, or to mark a change in level, such as the potential danger of a single step.

Selection of contrasting materials need not be restricted to paving alone. For instance, the contrast between a smooth footpath and a rough-faced wall can be very attractive. This illustrates the point that the landscape design process is at its best when it embraces all the separate elements that make up a composition.

Sense of unity

Materials that complement each other can be used to create a sense of harmony, relaxation and comfort.

A single material like stone, high-quality pre-cast concrete or brick, used for paving, steps and walls can create a pleasing sense of unity. Alternatively, unity can be achieved by linking together a range of complementary materials, each chosen for a specific function, but with, for example, a common colour or texture.

The concept of unity can be extended to the formation of visual links between indoor and outdoor spaces. Slate, brick and ceramic tiles can also achieve this, as illustrated.

Shade on pavings

The dazzling sun and prolonged heat of Southern Europe makes summer shade highly valued. Although Britain experiences the pleasure less often, dappled patterns of shade on paving, changing by the hour and season, can nevertheless

Figure 2.5 The richness of contrasting textures is best appreciated at close quarters.

Figure 2.6 Contrasting paving can be used to create interest in larger spaces and indicate priority routes.

Figure 2.7 The use of a single material for walls, paving and steps creates a pleasing sense of unity.

Figure 2.8 Dappled shade adds a constantly changing texture and can enliven spatial quality.

make a pleasing contrast to the man-made elements within a sunny, open space. Foliage overhead should not be too dense – trees with a comparatively open branch structure, like plane, birch or false acacia are to be preferred. In winter, the fine tracery of bare branches is a delight.

The careful relationship of buildings to the spaces between them can help to ensure that winter sun reaches at least some of the 'floor' for part of the day, minimizing the negative effects of dense shade such as wet, slippery pavings and poor plant growth.

Arcades on the south sides of buildings combine protected routes with summer shade and winter shelter. In Britain, their depth should be limited to allow sunlight to penetrate.

Important footpaths, ramps or steps are best sited away from deep shade, in order to reduce the growth of slippery algae on them. It is also essential to ensure good drainage of all paved surfaces, so that water does not accumulate.

Light reflection from pavings

Darker, less light-reflective, materials suit situations where the paving needs to be unobtrusive, although care should be taken to avoid creating paved spaces which have a gloomy winter character. Dark pavings are useful for reducing summer glare where people walk or sit or children play and for areas overlooked by large south-facing windows where there is no shade relief. Conversely, the reflectivity of light-coloured paving can help to brighten dark surroundings.

Gradients, crossfalls and contours

Gradients are an important aspect of paving design, but care must be taken to provide adequate drainage as well as the proper visual integration of the paving with the setting. Slopes can be used to emphasize the relationship between paved surfaces and buildings, or between one space and another. Paths should generally blend with the contours and not detract from the natural ground features, crossing contours obliquely rather than at right angles to avoid uncomfortable gradients. Unnatural, steep cuttings on banks can be avoided by incorporating generous adjustments to adjoining slopes or banks. Local recontouring is sometimes necessary either to achieve the desired gradient, or to conceal a footpath from specific viewpoints.

Crossfalls are essential for good drainage, and this is discussed in more detail later in this chapter. Generally, the coarser and more permeable paving materials should have somewhat steeper gradients than those necessary for smoother and more watertight finishes. The difficulties that gradients may pose

a)

b)

c)

d)

Figure 2.9 Shade falling on paving as a) relief in an open landscape, b) the contrast of deep shade, or c) dappled shade on a large area of town paving helps reduce glare and breaks the uniformity of the space, although d) unrelieved shade from buildings can create cold and slippery surfaces.

Figure 2.10   Paths should generally cross the contours obliquely to avoid uncomfortable gradients or ugly scars.

for the elderly, the disabled and people pushing prams or trolleys must be taken into account in the design.

Paving Construction

Durability and loadbearing

It is important to take account of the anticipated wear and loading when selecting paving materials, because the durability and strength of various paving materials varies quite widely. The underlying base and sub-base transmit loadings to the subsoil below with the overall depth of construction depending on the function of the paving and the nature of the sub-soil. Heavier vehicles clearly require a greater depth of construction than paths for pedestrians. There are a number of excellent publications, some of which are listed in the Bibliography, which concentrate on the construction aspects of pavings. Do not hesitate to seek further technical advice whenever necessary both from engineers and from manufacturers.

Trim

Kerbs or edgings are essential for most paving materials. Their functions include:

- preventing lateral movement of the paving materials, or of those that creep, like asphalts and coated macadams;
- warning to pedestrians (who may be blind or partially sighted) against stepping into the road and oncoming vehicles;
- preventing vehicles encroaching onto a footpath or area of planting;
- helping to channel water into the surface water drainage system;
- demarcation between materials to indicate different uses;
- demarcation between paving and adjoining planting.

Materials used for this purpose include pre.cast concrete kerbs, ranging from the normal roadside kerbs to narrow kerbs used to edge paths; precast concrete paving blocks; bricks and specially-shaped brick paviors; stone or stone setts, and timber.

Materials such as timber and galvanized mild steel strip may be used for edgings where only light use is anticipated. Timber edging is normally secured with stout timber pegs at about 1.0m centres. Smooth curves can be formed if vertical saw cuts are made at close centres in the back of the boards, so that they can be bent. Pressure-impregnated softwoods are usually used and this is a relatively economic solution for lightly used paved areas. While more substantial timber sections make attractive informal edgings, they are costly and can only be used in straight lengths.

Surface drainage

Many paving surfaces are impervious, or nearly so. Even materials which are initially porous gradually become clogged with fine silt; therefore, in order to remove water rapidly from paved areas, it is necessary to provide adequate

Table 2.1   Normal falls or slopes for the main paving materials

Surface	Crossfall	Longfall
concrete	1 in 60 straight crossfall	1 in 100 or 150
bituminous or	1 in 40 camber	1 in 200
tar surfacing	1 in 40 straight crossfall	
	1 in 60 in playgrounds	
gravel	1 in 30	
paving slabs	1 in 60 is commonly specified	
	Successful traditional practice suggests more generous falls could be used, without danger of slipperiness	
public pavements	1 in 40 and 1 in 30 are common, and other crossfalls may be common locally. Check with local authority	

Figure 2.11   A well-defined edging which enhances the planting, as well as protecting it from encroaching vehicles.

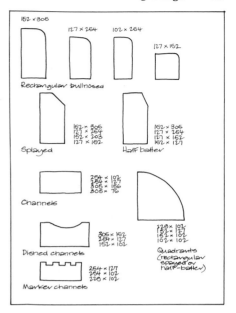

Figure 2.12   Range of precast concrete edgings and channels, with nominal dimension sizes.

gradients to drainage channels or to gulleys which carry the surface water away. It is good practice to design pavings so that they slope away from the foot of buildings, to avoid ponding at doorways and damp walls. Sometimes, small areas of paving can be laid to fall towards adjacent grass or planted areas, but this is not a practical solution, unless the ground is really well drained.

The design of falls in an area of paving depends on its size, materials and the proposed drainage system. Footpaths are usually laid to a single crossfall over their width, draining to a continuous channel or to adjacent porous soil. On long slopes, where the gradient is steeper than the crossfall, intercepting cross-channels are necessary, particularly for unbound materials.

In order to assess the number and location of drainage channels and gulleys required in larger areas of paving, the designer either works from personal experience, or calculates from local rainfall statistics. The falls are then arranged to create appropriate catchment areas.

Falls to a single gulley placed centrally in a paved area create a dished hollow which may flood if the gulley becomes blocked. Moreover not only is it a disturbing solution visually if repeated over a large paved area, but it is also expensive if used with larger-sized precast concrete slab paving, as a considerable number of diagonal cuts are required. Laying the paving from a central crown to peripheral drains is generally a more successful solution in broad areas of paving. Complex changes in gradients are easier to achieve in small unit pavings or homogeneous materials.

Falls are also necessary along the length of open channels, towards the gulleys. These are comparatively simple to form if the channel is constructed of unit paving made of brick or concrete paving or stone setts. Alternatively, there are precast concrete channels available that take up the longitudinal fall below ground within the concrete section, which simplify falls on paved areas.

Channels and gulleys

Gulley gratings must be strong enough to take occasional heavy point loads and allow easy access for routine cleaning. They are generally manufactured in

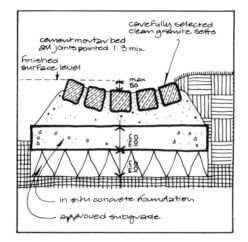

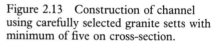

Figure 2.13   Construction of channel using carefully selected granite setts with minimum of five on cross-section.

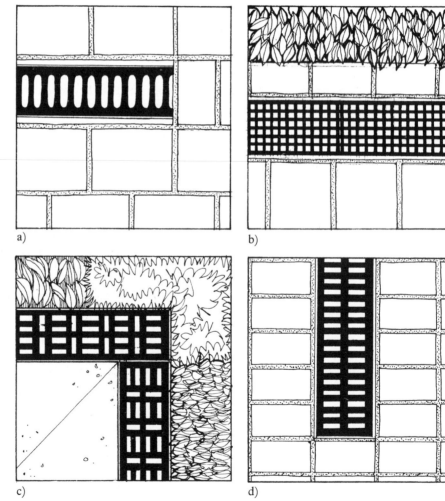

Figure 2.14   Proprietary metal gratings for pedestrian-only zones; a) straight bar, b) square mesh, c) transverse slot, d) twin slot.

precast concrete, cast iron and galvanized steel. They are available in various shapes and sizes suitable for most situations, with a variety of aperture patterns. With precast concrete channels in particular, the apertures in the slabs over the channels should not be too narrow, otherwise they are likely to be blocked by debris. Neither must they act as heel traps.

Since the positioning and treatment of channels and gulleys can enhance or mar the appearance of a paved area, their detailed design requires very careful consideration. Square or rectangular gratings should be aligned with paving bonding pattern or, in an homogenous surface, with nearby features such as walls, fences or steps. Circular gulleys should be avoided in areas of unit paving, as they are difficult to marry in without unsightly cutting, but they are well-suited to areas of continuous-surface materials such as rolled gravel.

Frames for gulleys and channels are secured in position by being haunched up in mortar. The haunching should not extend to the surface as it would break the visual relationship between the gulley and surrounding paving materials. Where there is insufficient depth for the normal paving material and bed, brick or precast concrete 'slips' can be used to carry the paving right up to the gulley.

Surface water destinations

It is necessary to determine whether the surface water can discharge into a sewer, soakaway or water course of sufficient capacity, and whether the surface water is likely to be contaminated with oil, in which case silt traps and oil interceptors may be necessary. Consult the local authority and the relevant water authority if any change to an existing drainage regime is anticipated. Because the design of underground surface drainage water systems is a complex matter in its own right, it has not been included in this Guide, but the Bibliography indicates useful sources of information.

Figure 2.15 Concrete drainage channels integrated with concrete block paving.

Figure 2.16 Alternative metal gulleys suitable for different paving materials. Examples show, a) square dished in precast slabs, b) round dished in in-situ concrete, c) round flat in cobbles, d) square slotted in brick.

Underground services

Although out of sight, underground services and their location are an important consideration in the successful implementation and management of landscaped areas.

It is important to develop the landscape design in conjunction with the services layout, so that the service runs and inspection chambers are located where they least disrupt the overall design. A good solution, in new developments, is the adoption of a common service trench, although this can be difficult to achieve in practice because it requires the coordinated action of all service authorities. A more flexible arrangement is the reservation of service corridors within which all installations are routed. This corridor should be located beneath grass which can be designed to coincide with road verges and sightlines needed for safety reasons, or below low-growing shrubs, which can be easily reinstated. Trees should be planted at sufficient distance from a service reservation to avoid future damage to the mature root systems during repair excavations. The landscape architect should be asked to advise on this technical question.

Ugly scars across hard surfaces can be caused by allowing random access for repair or extension of scattered underground services especially where heavy vehicles are routinely used. Strong unit paviors laid on a flexible base, can minimize the reinstatement scars.

A frequent cause of paving failure after service installations or repairs is inadequate consolidation of backfilling of excavated materials to service trenches, so that it continues to settle for several years. This can be avoided by using hard inorganic material, placed in well-consolidated layers in accordance with good engineering practice.

The landscape architect and services engineer should coordinate the location and type of proposed access or manhole covers in relation to vehicle loading so that the correct grade may be selected to avoid dangerous failure or fracture (see BS 497, Part 1: 1976). The choice of cover shapes should be determined by the surrounding paving. Square or rectangular covers suit rectangular unit paving and should be positioned to follow the direction of the bond line. Much unsightly cutting is necessary to fit unit pavings around circular covers, and these are best used in flowing surfaces such as tarmacadam or gravel. Recessed covers, which can be infilled with most types of paving materials, allow the cover and the surrounding paving to merge visually.

The final success of a scheme depends as much upon adequate site supervision as upon the initial design coordination. Covers must be installed flush with surrounding paving to avoid ugly and dangerous changes of level. Most inspection covers can be quite easily constructed to align with a sloping surface as steep as 1:2, if necessary. The frame supporting a cover has to be haunched with mortar but this should not be visible at the surface.

A common fault that frequently occurs as a result of poor design and inaccurate setting out is when a cover straddles the boundary of two materials, instead of lying wholly within one of them. Once drains or other services are installed it may be difficult to move the inspection cover more than a small amount and it is often too late to adjust the paving design, except at considerable expense.

It is helpful if underground services are indicated by discreet, flush surface markers. A random scattering of unrelated inspection covers, ugly marker posts, notices and control boxes can easily overwhelm the most carefully thought-out landscape design. Although markers must be clearly visible for emergency use,

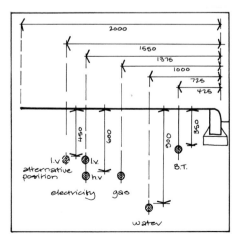

Figure 2.17 Nominal positions for utilities beneath a public pavement. Although this arrangement is widely adopted, the relevant authorities must be consulted before excavation.

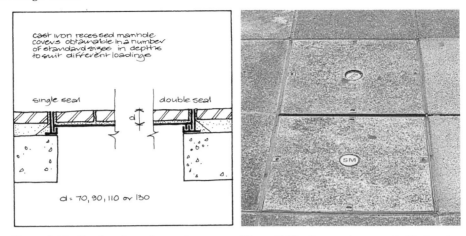

Figure 2.18   Section through cast-iron recessed manhole cover.

Figure 2.19   Recessed covers, infilled and positioned to match surrounding paving.

they do not need to be free-standing if the plates giving their location can be fitted to existing posts, or adjacent walls. This type of marker is less vulnerable to damage and less likely to cause an obstruction.

Finally, account should be taken of the particular access requirements of specialist equipment or vehicles for subsequent maintenance work on underground services.

Trees in paving

In order to preserve existing trees in an area of new paving, the following points should be observed:

1.   Maintain existing ground levels within the spread of the canopy and avoid cutting the roots.
2.   Retain a porous zone around the tree, over as large an area as possible, to facilitate good aeration and drainage. This zone allows fertilizers to be applied and watering to be carried out as necessary.
3.   Prevent soil contamination by oil, petrol etc., or compaction by heavy machinery or storage of materials within the canopy spread during construction.
4.   Install a raised kerb around trees planted in car parks to ensure that polluted surface water is directed away from the roots.

When new trees are planted in paving, provision must always be made for an adequate volume of topsoil and for root aeration. The minimum openings in paving for new trees is about 900mm in diameter.

Standard tree grilles are generally available in cast iron, galvanized steel or precast concrete. Sizes vary from 900mm square, to approximately 1,800mm. They may also be square or circular. These grilles must be strong enough to take the weight of small maintenance vehicles used in tree care and in sweeping, and have sufficient open area to serve the needs of the tree roots. Their thickness depends on the loads expected, the span and the type of material being used. For cast iron, a typical thickness is 25mm, for steel about 20mm and for precast concrete 50mm. They are normally made in two or more sections for ease of installation and removal for occasional sweeping. When more than two sections are used, a central support is required to prevent collapse. Some grilles allow greater flexibility in that the central sections can be removed as tree growth increases. The steel frame of the grille is supported by the foundation of the paving trim that abuts the grille in order to keep it flush with the paving.

Where it is necessary, in urban areas, to protect tree trunks from accidental damage by vehicles, circular metal tree guards can conveniently be anchored to the framework of the tree grille or, less obtrusively, bollards may be placed on the sides where vehicles may intrude.

It is important to prevent the soil from becoming compacted within openings for trees where grilles are not used. Bricks, or setts, laid on a sand bed, are commonly used as a finish. In places where they are unlikely to be used as missiles, other materials such as loose cobbles may be appropriate. All of these materials may be removed as the tree grows.

Design Elements

Multi-use paved areas

While ordinary roads protect and separate pedestrians from the greater speed and mass of vehicles by means of a kerb, there are circumstances where the two can safely share the same surface. The essential prerequisites are that the vehicles move slowly – that is, not more than two or three times normal walking pace – and that the areas shared with vehicles are always clearly defined from areas designated purely for pedestrians.

The careful siting of bollards, lighting and other street furniture can also help to reinforce people's safety in vehicle zones. Warning signs within the paved surface may also be required.

The design should accommodate the likely flow of people, and the construction should meet the loading, speed and frequency of vehicle use. The aim should be to achieve the right balance between the safe and pleasant use of the same space by pedestrians, including children playing on their own and handicapped people, as well as meeting the requirements for emergency and delivery vehicle carriageway width and turning circles.

Where the area of frequent vehicle movement can be defined it could be delineated by a change of surface colour and texture, or by level by the introduction of kerbs. With care, these provisions need not destroy the cohesion of a design but rather enhance it.

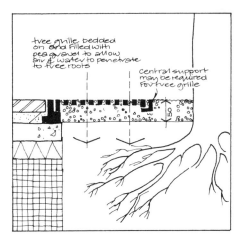

Figure 2.20 Representative section through tree pit showing position of grille.

Figure 2.21   Where pedestrians and vehicles meet, areas of multiple use should be made clearly visible. The paving must be designed to take occasional vehicular loads with any restrictions on access clearly defined.

Footpaths

The width of footpaths should relate to the intensity of their use and the need to accommodate the needs of the elderly, those on foot, the disabled and people pushing wheelchairs or prams. A large wheelchair requires a path width of at least 950mm, a person on crutches, 850mm, and a person with a stick, 750mm. Obstacles to movement, such as seats and lighting columns, should be offset from the path to give full clearance. Typical footpath widths vary from about 1,000mm, which allows two people to pass or the passage of a single wheelchair, to 1,800mm which allows two people with prams to pass each other. Where intensive use is anticipated, much wider paths are necessary.

The nature of the paved surface has a significant influence on safety, particularly for the disabled whose wheelchairs, for example, can become jammed in wide joints. Everyone is in danger of losing their footing in winter, so the steeper sloping surfaces should be non-slip (see pp. 12 and 14 for gradients). Pedestrian routes should always be free of motor traffic, unless constructed to take the weight of occasional utility or maintenance vehicles.

Steps

Outdoor steps should be comfortable to use, with consistent treads and risers in any one flight. Risers should not exceed about 150mm in height for regular use, or be shallower than 75mm. Generally, treads should not be less than about 300mm, with 450mm to 500mm being a more comfortable width. Treads greater than 500mm need to be designed to accommodate a normal stride.

Figure 2.22   A skilful transition from ramp to steps, accentuating the gradient.

Since so much depends on function and context, each situation should be assessed separately. For example, in a large-scale public place where the emphasis is on leisure, steps may be made very shallow, with 100mm risers and treads of 450–500mm. Elizabeth Beazley's *Design and Detail of the Space between Buildings* gives useful examples of steps in harmony with their surroundings. Where it does not significantly conflict with comfort and safety, the relationship of the riser to the tread may also be adjusted to suit the average slope of the natural surroundings.

A flight should generally have not less than three steps. On long flights there should be no more than fourteen treads between intermediate landings. The minimum width of flights of stairs for public access is 1,200mm, but in private areas they can be narrower, down to about 750mm.

Since steps may be used by the elderly or shortsighted, at least one handrail or guiding wall should be provided, and one on each side where the width exceeds 1,200mm. Handrails must be provided for any public flight of steps. The height should be not less than 840mm or more than 1,000mm, measured vertically above the nosing. On wide flights they must be no further apart than 3.0m centres. Where there is a danger of injury from failing to see the front edge of the steps, the nosings should be in white or a light colour.

Good lighting is necessary for the safe use of steps at night and can be successfully incorporated into the flank walls or risers (see Chapter 21 'Lighting – the night landscape').

Good surface drainage is essential to discourage the formation of ice on treads, causing slipperiness as well as possible frost failure. Treads should have a slight forward slope so that water is shed but care should be taken to ensure that steps do not become a drainage channel for a larger area of paving. Surface water from the paving at the top of the flight should fall away from the upper step or a drainage channel, perhaps covered by a grating, should be provided across the top. The area at the foot of the steps should also be well drained.

All steps must be structurally stable, including those of informal character made with timber risers used to support gravel treads. However, for steps of stone or brick a sound concrete foundation with an adequate toe is essential,

Figure 2.23a   Timber risers supporting gravel treads suit an informal, rural setting.

Figure 2.23b   Steps constructed of bricks often suit a formal, urban situation.

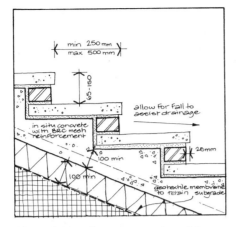

Figure 2.24a   Step construction with p.c. concrete slab as tread and brick risers.

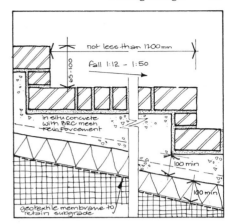

Figure 2.24b   Preferred construction for ramped slope, shown here faced in brick.

Figure 2.25   Cobbles and stone flags combine to create an attractive flight of steps.

Figure 2.26 *Above:* Shallow steps used as a dramatic element in the Pirelli garden at the Victoria and Albert Museum.

Figure 2.27 *Right:* A method of intercepting surface water above steps.

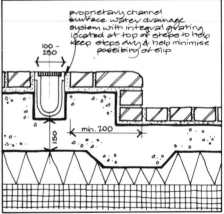

particularly for flights on clayey soils, made-up ground or where they form part of a structure retaining a slope. In any of these conditions, civil engineering advice ought to be sought.

To reduce groundwater seepage that can leach lime from the concrete supporting structure outwards so that it stains brick or stone facings, drainage beneath the level of all concrete construction is necessary. As an additional precaution, the concrete substructure can be coated with a bituminous damp-proofing material. While this is still tacky, sharp sand is applied to provide a key for the mortar bedding of the material forming the treads and risers.

A firm leading edge is essential for steps subjected to heavy use, since this is where maximum wear can be expected. Soft bricks liable to crumble after repeated frosts can be a real danger and should be avoided. Whatever material is used, a slightly rounded nosing reduces chipping and retains a crisp appearance. A slip-resistant surface is desirable, particularly on a long flight of steps or where there is likely to be much leaf fall. Solid steps of hard stone, such as sawn granite, not only offer a sound and frostproof surface but contribute greatly towards an atmosphere of high quality and permanence.

Cleaning steps – an important safety factor – can be achieved by installing a cleaning channel at one side, preferably beneath a handrail to avoid twisted ankles! Emergency fire exits should have an outside landing, not less than 1,500mm deep, before any steps are reached.

Ramps

Ramps are an essential alternative to steps for prams, trolleys and wheelchairs, and should be comfortable to use. In practice, this means limiting the gradient to between, say, 1:15 and 1:20 for distances over 3.0m, although for shorter lengths, slopes up to 1:10 are acceptable. The recommended maximum gradient for wheelchairs is 1:12, with a maximum length of 6m between resting places. The preferred gradient is 1:20, with resting points every 10m. By making the resting points turning circles as well, it is possible to discourage cycle-racing or roller-skating. Ramps must have an effective barrier at the bottom if they open on to roads. Handrails and adequate lighting are necessary in most situations and textured surfaces help to ensure a good grip in wet or icy weather.

Stepped ramps are an intermediate solution, which can be used where steps would cause an undesirable concentration in the contours and a ramp would be too steep for comfortable access. In *Design and Detail of the Space between Buildings*, Elizabeth Beazley suggests allowing for an odd number – say, three paces – on each tread.

The next six chapters discuss the quality of the more important paving materials, starting with natural stone.

Figure 2.28   *Left:* Preferred dimensions for ramped access suitable for wheelchairs.

Figure 2.29   *Right:* A ramp paved with traditional materials.

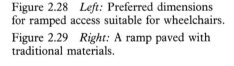

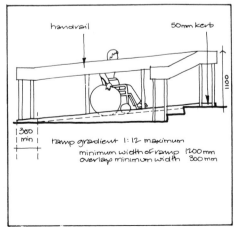

CHAPTER 3

Natural Stone

Stone is available as paving slabs, kerbs, setts and cobbles and, in loose form, as crushed rock or gravels.

Stone Paving Slabs

A decline in the use of natural stone is due largely to the comparatively high costs arising from the skill required for its preparation and the high level of craftsmanship required in the final laying. This is compounded for most new paving slabs by high transport costs from upland Britain to the lowlands, where the major demand occurs. Finally, most substitute products, while lacking the original qualities of real stone, have proved reliable in use over many years and significantly cheaper to purchase, as well as being more uniform and therefore easier and cheaper to lay.

However, there are certainly occasions where stone can, and should, be used – for example, where the highest-quality finishes can be justified, to match an existing area of natural stone paving, or to integrate paving with a stone-faced building or stone walls.

Stone paving is most appropriate in its place of origin, where its uses and laying techniques have evolved in close response to need. Using a particular stone in another geological area – for example, using limestone in an area where granite or slate predominates – will inevitably produce an incongruous solution. Within large cities, like London, the use of a wide range of building stone has become an established tradition. Their qualities continue to be appreciated.

Natural stone is a finite resource and the decision to use it should be carefully considered. The stripping of the natural limestone upland pavements in the north of England for rock gardens across the country, is a sad example of landscape destruction.

Advice on stone supplies and contracting services may be obtained from the Stone Federation who publish a *Handbook* and *Directory*.

Types of paving stone

Deposits of building stone occur over much of the north and west of the British Isles, but not all are suitable for paving. Slab sizes vary according to the inherent strength and weight of particular types of stone, as noted below, and vary even in different seams from the same quarry. The maximum size in York stone or slate is about 900 x 600mm, although slate may be available in larger sizes, which have to be thicker to overcome handling stresses.

All stone that has natural bedding planes, laid down at the time of its formation, should be laid at approximately the same angle to minimize the

Figure 3.1   *Left:* Stone paving is most appropriate in its place of origin.

Figure 3.2   *Right:* Riven slate offers a texture which blends sympathetically with other natural materials, as well as subtle colours.

possibility of frost damage caused by water being drawn by gravity or capillary action and then freezing: this eventually causes the stone to split (see also BS 5390: 1976).

The most readily available stones for paving slabs are:

- *Sandstone:* York stone is a fine-grained type of sandstone which can be finished with a riven, sawn or rubbed surface. The colour ranges from creamy white through light buff to brown, and the thickness varies between 50 and 70mm, depending on the overall size of the slab. Similar stone is available from Lancashire and the Forest of Dean, although in the latter case the stone is not available as riven slabs.
- *Granite:* Quarried in Scotland and Cornwall, granite is heavy, hardwearing and very slow to weather. Because it is dense, weight usually restricts the size of slab although the development of mechanized handling plant has considerably reduced this constraint. Its colour varies from grey/white through red to blue/grey and black, depending upon the area of the country and strata from which the stone has been quarried. Imported granite is available from Belgium, Norway and Portugal.
- *Slate:* This is almost as hardwearing and as slow to weather as granite, but is rather brittle. The colour ranges from 'slate grey' through blue/greys and purples to green, depending on whether it is quarried in Cumbria, Wales or Cornwall. Smaller slates are usually riven but larger sizes can be sawn, planed or fine-rubbed. Finely rubbed finishes are best limited to benches or tables, as they become extremely slippery when wet, riven or sawn textures being preferable for paving. Riven small unit paviors may be only 10–12mm thick. Slate slabs of 25–30mm thick are usual, although thicknesses of up to 70mm may be available. The greater thicknesses allow the material to be used in the large slabs required at the scale of important urban squares.

- *Limestone:* This comes from three main sources, quite different in character. Portland Stone is generally white or grey in colour and is readily available in sawn or rubbed finishes. Purbeck Stone is generally harder and more expensive. Bath Stone (white to light brown in colour) is not hardwearing and should be used externally only for lightly trafficked areas. Limestone slabs are usually 50–65mm thick.

In addition to newly cut stone, natural stone paving can often be obtained second-hand. Inner-city clearance over the last thirty years or so has thrown up a good source of salvaged materials, including York stone slabs. Some local authorities have architectural salvage schemes and store recovered materials.

A useful reference for selecting an appropriate stone is the *Natural Stone Directory,* compiled and published by The Stone Industries, which describes the sources, geology, and applications of most stone quarried in Great Britain. Price guides should be consulted for information on relative costs of buying and of transport.

Texture

Typical finishes are riven, sawn, tooled or rubbed. They vary in cost, reflecting the skills and labour involved. Riven natural stone slabs generally make a very durable and traditional form of paving. Patterning with horizontal grooves is often used to improve grip on ramps or steps.

Construction

Although durable, natural stone flags can be brittle, so they must be supported by a thoroughly consolidated base. This is blinded, then overlaid with a 25mm

Figure 3.3   Stone has traditionally been used in formal garden design.

bed of dry 1:6 to 1:5 cement:sand mortar or 1:3 to 1:4 lime:sand mortar, on to which the flags are placed and carefully tamped into position until well bedded. The depth of dry mortar allows irregularities in the thickness of the slabs to be accommodated.

Joints between slabs are usually filled with cement or lime mortar, which is appropriate for formal or urban settings. In rural or garden settings open joints or wider gaps may be preferred, to allow prostrate plants to grow between the flags.

Design

Paving patterns should reflect the characteristics of the stone used. The most natural pattern makes the best use of the characteristics of the stone, consistent with good design – for instance, random-squared York stone. For greater formality, the width may be coursed at, say, 600mm with random lengths. Generally speaking, formal, regular slabs complement formal spaces.

To create an open design of attractive proportions, stone slabs can be laid within a matrix of other materials, such as bricks or gravel. This can be a more economic use of this costly material where the budget is restricted, and is also a means of introducing extra visual interest.

Stone Setts and Kerbs

During the Industrial Revolution, setts became the normal multi-purpose paving surface in the rapidly expanding cities, because of their durability, coupled with

Figure 3.4   Open-jointed stone sett paving with colonizing plants.

Figure 3.5   White concrete blocks are inserted to provide road markings in the stone sett paving of this thoroughfare.

the relative cheapness of labour, at that time, for cutting and laying. They were cut from the nearest suitable stone – granite, hard limestone, whinstone, basalt, or sandstone. Nowadays, granite is virtually the only stone sett in commercial production, mainly imported from Spain and Portugal.

Setts, particularly granite, are very durable, and most supplies available now are salvaged materials. Second-hand setts should be specified as 'cleaned and ready to lay'.

New and second-hand stone kerbs are also made from granite or whinstone and are attractive and extremely durable. Old granite kerbs can be re-used to form steps or substantial edgings to paving or planting. Dressed natural stone kerbs, channels, quadrants and setts are prepared to the dimensions in BS 435:1975.

Artificial textured concrete setts can fulfil many of the usual roles of stone setts, although they lack such interesting random variations in texture and colour. On the other hand, in pedestrian areas with heavy foot traffic, their greater smoothness and low cost can make them a sensible choice.

Characteristics

Natural stone setts are very variable in size, depending on source. There is also much greater variation within size classes than with manufactured materials. The depth of setts usually varies from 100mm to 150mm. Typical sizes on plan are: 100 x 100mm, 100 x 125mm, 125 x 125mm, 100 x 150mm, 125 x 150mm, 150 x 150mm, 100 x 200mm, and larger sizes are sometimes available. It is worthwhile checking the locally available sizes before incorporating setts into a design.

The texture of setts varies from coarse-grained granite to smooth whinstone, but the texture overall depends upon the way the joints are designed. Joints filled with coarse sand allow water and air to reach tree roots in paved areas.

Figure 3.6   Commonly used patterns and bonds for setts. a) stack, b) stretcher, c) circular, d) fan.

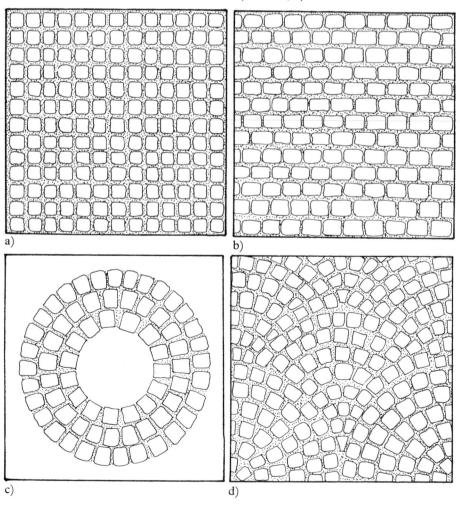

a)

b)

c)

d)

Figure 3.7 Suitable shapes and sizes for specific functions can be selected from the ranges of cobble sizes available. Here two sizes are used to delineate between vehicular space and a transition zone.

Construction

For pedestrian use, the setts are laid on a 25mm sand bed on a 100mm well-consolidated base. The setts should be well rammed and the joints filled with lime mortar brushed in dry and then well watered. Where setts are used for steps and edgings, they must be bedded in mortar. Where subjected to vehicular use, they should be supported on normal road construction. Some setts are neatly trimmed, allowing a good interlock, while others are rough-edged and so require wider joints. Very careful selection and laying are necessary.

Setts should be laid with the bedding planes of the stone aligned vertically to prevent deterioration or frost damage. They can be laid on moderate slopes, up to 1:12. Their rough surface texture and frequent joints provide a good grip underfoot but, in order to drain effectively, there should be a generous crossfall. Setts can be laid on steeper slopes, such as on a facing to a low retaining wall.

Design

The variety of sizes of setts allows considerable flexibility and complexity in design. Square setts can be laid stack bond, stretcher bond or, with greater craftsmanship, in a curved or fan pattern. The fan pattern is best set out in the traditional way by a man sitting on a low stool and laying the setts radially around himself. Rectangular setts are usually laid stretcher-bond. The scale of the space should determine the scale of the pattern to be used. For example, the gentle flow of the fan pattern needs a large, uninterrupted area for it to be expressed adequately, while stack bond quickly loses its impact in a large space.

Sett paving for pedestrian use should have a flush wearing surface. Damaged, second-hand setts can still be used for borders, edgings and rumble strips.

Because of their relatively small size, setts work well with other materials. They can be used within a larger pattern, which helps to increase the perceived

Figure 3.8   Alternating bands of natural stone cobbles and granite are combined to create an unusual ramp feature.

scale or, conversely, to form a framework of grey granite setts around larger expanses of stone or concrete paving slabs.

In addition to paving large areas, setts are often used in small quantities for special purposes. They make an excellent edging for other materials, such as tarmac or gravel where they meet grass or planting. They can be laid to form drainage channels or low steps. The rough texture of a strip of setts, say 2–5 units wide, can be used to delineate easily visible boundaries between activities. A wider band provides an effective rumble strip in areas where pedestrians and slow-moving cars are mingled.

Cobbles

No manufactured product can compare with the appearance of a cobbled space. The flexibility, toughness and rich diversity of this natural material makes it a valuable element in paving design.

For centuries, cobbles have been incorporated into urban and rural paving in a casual and informal way, no doubt because of their ready availability. Streets were paved with the flatter cobbles, particularly in waterside communities where a supply was immediately to hand, from beach or river. There are some very fine examples of large areas of cobbles laid and maintained over many centuries without serious deterioration, bearing witness to their lasting qualities when they are well laid.

Traditionally, cobbles were used for multi-purpose paving. Because the roughness of a cobbled surface suits horses but is not ideal for pedestrians or vehicles, the main tracks were surfaced with stone slabs, with cobbles providing a relatively inexpensive means of infilling the irregular areas on either side. Because they are difficult to walk across, the larger and rounded cobbles can provide a most effective and subtle means of directing pedestrians.

Cobbles harmonize well with other local, natural materials. For example, knapped or split flints look well where they are also used for adjacent walling. However, the coarse texture of cobbles does tend to trap dirt and litter and so requires a higher standard of maintenance.

Figure 3.9 Cobbles can be used as effective edging strips.

Figure 3.10 The varied shapes of cobbles allow great freedom of design.

Characteristics

Since cobbles are water-formed, their shape varies from being flat, rounded or egg-shaped with considerable variation in colour. Before deciding on a specification for cobbled surfaces it is as well to establish local availability of colour, size and shape. The usual size gradings (maximum diameter) are: up to 35mm; 35–50mm; 75–100mm; 100–125mm; 125mm plus.

Construction

For pedestrian areas, cobbles should be laid by pressing them into a 50mm bed of small aggregate concrete on a 75mm well consolidated base. Where vehicles are expected, the above must be laid on a suitable road base. The most satisfactory appearance is achieved by laying them so that they touch, with the larger end down. Good workmanship and supervision are essential, because the work depends on skill in selecting the cobbles and laying them to ensure that they fit well one with the other. Cobbles set in mortar can considerably impede the flow of water, so they should be laid to a fall of at least 1 in 30.

Where cobbles are lifted, perhaps because of a need to repair underground services, it is usually difficult to conceal the disturbance unless they are relaid carefully. If access is anticipated, manholes and ducts should be provided with recessed metal covers, filled with cobbles bedded in mortar.

In a private garden or institution, where there is no risk of their being used as projectiles, cobbles can be laid loose. Generous coverage of the ground with cobbles, laid on perforated black PVC sheeting can effectively suppress weeds. They are a good material to place around trees where, like grilles, they allow the passage of air and water.

Design

The cost of using cobbles nowadays is high. Unless laid flat, they do not constitute a suitable walking surface, and then they can be slippery when wet or icy. However, their strong visual texture and traditional associations make them a desirable material in a number of situations, for example:

a) to form a transition between a building and an unrelated paving material around it;
b) to provide a suitable immediate setting for sculptures, fountains, memorials or other focal points;
c) to gently dissuade people from walking on a specific area in order to improve safety or enhance privacy;
d) to form a dished drainage channel;
e) to provide a contrast to smooth paving or walls.

The traditional pattern arises naturally from the method of laying them shoulder to shoulder, all orientated the same way, but fan, stretcher and herringbone patterns can also be achieved. The flexibility of size and colour allows the creation of designs such as emblems or initials within the cobbled area. Although an infinite number of variations is possible, designs can easily appear over-elaborate and out of scale if the space is large. In large areas, geometric patterns can be created by the selection of cobbles by size and colour to achieve simple, but striking, effects.

Figure 3.11   Gravel is an excellent informal surface for light traffic in private gardens and rural situations.

Gravel

Gravel production, from naturally occurring deposits, falls into two main classes:

1. by grading deposits through screens to provide building sand, aggregates and rejects or using materials as dug to provide hoggin and roadstones;
2. by washing, crushing and grading wet or dry deposits to provide graded aggregates.

A wide variety of materials are used in landscape construction and gravels are a well-tried and valued surfacing material, at home in rural or urban locations especially in their areas of origin.

Characteristics

Naturally occurring gravel beds are found in river basins and in glacial deposits. The water-worn material consists of rounded pebbles from river beds or from coastal deposits, often mixed with sands, and is available in a range of sizes.

'Pea shingle' is a uniform, rounded, single-sized gravel, typically around 6mm in diameter, which drains well but cannot be compacted to make a stable surface. In graded gravels, the particle sizes are specified by proportion and they include a high fraction of fine material and can thus be satisfactorily compacted to form a stable surface.

Hoggin, of which Breedon gravel is a type, is another naturally occurring excavated material which has self-binding properties. It has a clay fraction which helps to set the components hard when watered and rolled. For the treament of ordinary Hoggin see page 42.

Unbound gravel does require more maintenance than most other paving materials, including raking, weed removal and occasional topping-up.

The second source of gravel is crushed quarried rock. An angular material which is easily laid and interlocks well when compacted, it provides a good informal wearing surface. There are certain rocks which have self-binding properties, of which Breedon gravel is a well-known example. When laid, rolled and finally 'water rolled', they form a structurally sound pavement.

In Scotland, a commonly used local gravel material is 'blaes', an industrial waste product from the processing of oil shales.

Crushed stone is available in different grades from specific sources to provide a surface of uniform appearance. As with all types of stone, the cost is influenced by the haulage distances involved.

Gravels vary in colour from yellow ochre through brown to greys and even greens, such as Criggion stone.

Construction

A gravel surface must be laid on a well consolidated base, which spreads the load on to the formation level. The recommended falls for a gravel surface are 1:30 and these are incorporated into the formation level. Since rainwater can percolate through an unsealed gravel surface, it is desirable to provide subsoil drainage adjacent to the paved area so that the moisture content below remains reasonably constant. Steeper crossfalls generally lead to erosion and wash-out of the finer particles.

Heavy rolling is required at all stages of construction. If this is not done properly, then the surface can quickly become loose and unsatisfactory in use. Where vehicles are likely to cause heavy wear by turning or braking, the strength of the surface can be increased by incorporating a bituminous emulsion.

Figure 3.12   Two examples of gravel footpath construction with timber edging.

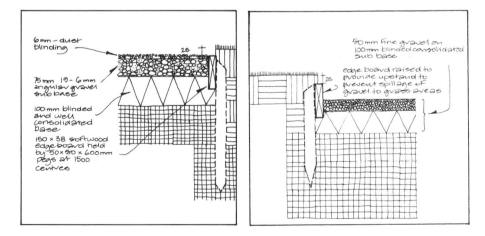

Figure 3.13 Steps with risers of a unit paving material, such as these bricks with treads of gravel, can achieve a successful transition between a formally paved area and an informal gravel path.

A more attractive solution is to give the gravel the surface stability of tarmacadam, using a colourless binder which allows the rich texture and warm colours of the stone to be seen.

Design

Gravel is an ideal surface finish for low-intensity or irregular use, especially for areas of shade under trees or building overhangs where grass cannot be expected to grow. It also makes a good finish to the soil below tree grilles.

Hoggin

Hoggin is a traditional surfacing material, composed of a naturally occurring mixture of gravel and clay, used for paths and lightly used private roads.

Characteristics

Hoggin makes an attractive, informal surface when properly laid. Its even, sandy-coloured appearance, coupled with the relative ease of construction and low capital cost, makes it an attractive material, provided that it is used in appropriate situations where its limitations are clearly understood. If it is subjected to heavy loading or severe pressure, as in sudden braking when wet, the surface can deteriorate into ruts and potholes.

Relative to other *in situ* pavings, hoggin has a short life, much depending upon its location and usage. Nevertheless, as it is easily repaired or relaid, it may, with good management, have a favourable cost-in-use figure.

Construction

Hoggin is laid over a well-consolidated base of appropriate thickness for the ground conditions and anticipated use. It is spread loosely and then compacted to a final depth of 100mm by rolling. Its major advantage is the ease with which it can be spread while still moist and before it is consolidated. After consolidation and drying out it becomes very firm.

The surface texture depends upon its gravel content and the range of stone sizes. Well-graded gravel helps the clay to bind on compaction. If very large pebbles appear on the surface, the clay cannot bind them; they should therefore

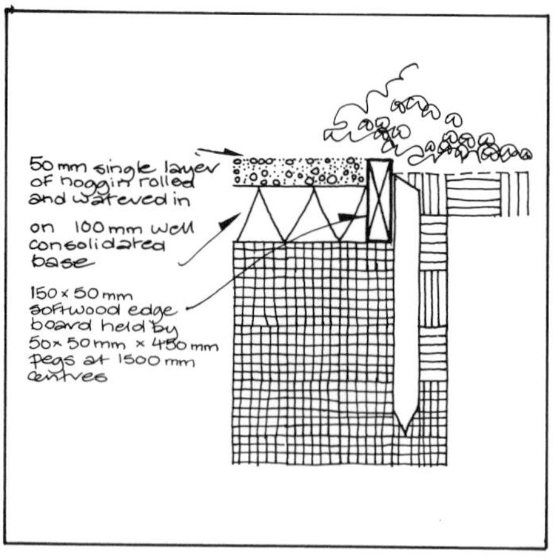

50 mm single layer of hoggin rolled and watered in

on 100 mm well consolidated base

150 x 50 mm softwood edge board held by 50 x 50 mm x 450 mm pegs at 1500 mm centres

Figure 3.14   Hoggin footpath construction with timber edging.

be removed, as they tend to break loose from the surface.

Hoggin depends on its own binding properties for its stability and suffers from erosion if surface water is allowed to run off too quickly. It should not therefore be laid on steep slopes where the fall is steeper than about 1:10. However, good surface drainage is necessary and the camber or crossfalls should not be less than 1:30.

If the surface is not used regularly, or if the formation level has not been sprayed with herbicide, weeds or grasses quickly establish and the hoggin gradually breaks down. In some instances – say, on either side of a clear central track – this may be in keeping with the desired informal character. Generally, however, it is necessary to control surface vegetation with herbicides. For more specific guidance on weed control see the Bibliography.

Figure 3.15 *Above:* Stone setts laid with a strongly defined edge and natural flagstone pavements.
Figure 3.16 *Right:* Gravel is an ideal surface for lightly used paths.

CHAPTER 4

Brick Paving

Clay bricks are one of the oldest forms of pavings, and they have been widely used wherever suitable clay has been available. Today, brick paving is as relevant and pleasing as it has ever been. The rich traditions of pattern and varied sources of individual clays give it a very special character. Brick pavers are durable, attractive and available in a wide range of colour, textures and sizes.

Characteristics

Some bricks intended for wall construction, (traditionally 212 x 105 x 65mm) can be used for paving. Only Category 'F' bricks, which can include engineering bricks and hard burnt stocks, are suitable for outdoor paving. In BS 3921:1985 'Specification for clay bricks', Category 'F' bricks are defined as being resistant to frost damage even when in a saturated condition and subjected to repeated cycles of freezing and thawing.

It is worth noting that high compressive strength and low water absorption in a brick are not always indicative of frost resistance. A brick with low compressive strength need not be discarded for use as a paver if it is highly frost-resistant. When contemplating the use of walling brick for paving, it is wise to confirm with the manufacturer that they are suitable for such an application.

Most brick manufacturers are now increasing their ranges of Category 'F' paver made for external use. Particular attention is given to the appearance of the upper face. The dimensions are designed for specific loadings and methods of laying. For flexible pavings there are two plan sizes – 200 x 100mm and 210 x 105mm – which are both available in two standard thicknesses, 50mm and 65mm. (See BS 6677 and 'A specification for clay pavers for flexible pavements', 2nd edition 1988, published by the Brick Development Association.) The edges may be chamfered, to reduce damage and improve surface grip, and spacer ridges may be moulded onto the sides, to ensure optimum spacing. Matching accessories such as kerbs, channels and starter units are available for some ranges of paver.

Pavers intended to be laid on a mortar base with mortar joints – that is, for rigid paving – are available in a wider range of sizes. Plan sizes are 215mm by 65, 102.5, 140 or 215mm, and thickness may be 33mm or 35mm (for pedestrian use only), 50mm or 65mm (for heavier loads). Mortar joint width will be 10mm (nominal) between pavers.

Brick pavers for flexible paving are categorized as either 'PA', suitable for pedestrian use, or as harder, denser and more uniform 'PB', for vehicular or industrial use where the traffic is moderate. Neither PA nor PB pavers readily absorb grime and dirt, so surface sealing is unnecessary and inadvisable.

Figure 4.1   Many brick pavers have matching accessories available.

Chemical cleaning of bricks by algicide or fungicide does not adversely affect them. Pavers may be cleaned by high pressure water jets, or by steam-cleaning.

There is a wide range of special-shaped bricks which allows designers to develop sophisticated and appropriate details. Standard specials (that is, those specials regularly available from manufacturers) are 'single or double bullnose' and 60° or 30° angle bricks for edging. However, because specials are usually fired separately, they may have a slightly different appearance or colour from the standard paving bricks and are naturally more expensive. Many manufacturers are prepared to quote for other specials.

Texture in brick pavers derives from the method of manufacture – that is, pressed, wire-cut, or hand-made. The first two produce a more consistent texture than the latter.

Some pressed pavers are closely related to engineering bricks and are manufactured to the same consistently high specification, although less dense. They are smooth-surfaced, so for external paving an impressed pattern is sometimes desirable – for example, diamond or chequered stable pavers, to improve traction.

Wire-cut or drag-faced pavers have a slightly roughened surface which helps to make them less slippery.

Hand-made bricks suitable for paving tend to be highly variable in form, texture and density and, as they are considerably more costly, should only be used where this quality is specifically required. For heavy-duty areas, whether pedestrian or vehicular, their resistance to surface abrasion should be checked with the manufacturer.

Variations in the texture and colour of paving bricks arise from different types of clay and the kiln firing conditions. As variation can also occur between batches, selection and mixing may be necessary at the factory for a large area of brick paving to distribute the different pavers reasonably evenly. The adoption of preferred brick and paver sizes helps designers to achieve continuity with adjoining buildings or walling. If it is necessary to mix bricks or pavers from different manufacturers, dimensional compatibility becomes important, and production sizes should be checked before ordering.

Construction

There are two methods of laying brick paving, flexible or rigid paving. Hybrids should be avoided.

Flexible construction

There is a long tradition of bedding pavers on coarse sand (to BS 882, Grade 'C'), known as 'flexible' construction. The details are clearly described in the 'Code of Practice for laying flexible pavements constructed in clay pavers (2nd edition 1988) published by the Brick Development Association and the County Surveyor's Society. The pavers are laid with close butt joints (2.0–5.0mm wide) filled with sand. A gap of this width is necessary to ensure that the sand grains, which create the bond by means of friction between the pavers, can enter. Flexible paving must be contained on all sides by an edge restraint, such as coordinated brick trims, bricks on edge, concrete kerbs, channels bedded and then haunched in concrete. The paving is compacted using a plate vibrator fitted with a rubber sole to avoid damage to the bricks, with an effective force of at least 75kN per square metre. After compaction, the surface is covered with dry sand (to BS 882, Grade 'F') brushed into joints and compacted again. Pavers should not be cut smaller than one-third of a whole unit, to prevent instability. The work should only be carried out in dry weather to avoid weak construction. Flexible brick paving is not self-draining, as the interstices soon fill up with detritus, and so must be laid to proper falls.

Rigid construction

Rigid brick paving is bedded on mortar and the joints (usually 10mm wide) are filled with mortar. The BDA recommendation for mortar is 1:1/4:3 cement:lime:sand to achieve good durability. The mortar joints should not exceed 10mm, to avoid cracking and an unpleasant overemphasis on joints in relation to the proportions of the paver. To prevent cracking in rigid paving, it

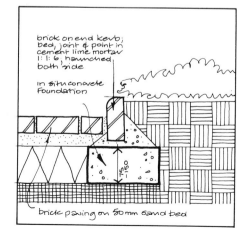

Figure 4.2　Rigid kerb detail for flexible brick paving.

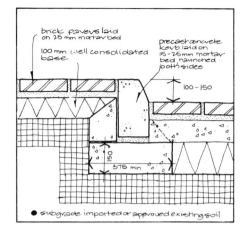

brick pavers laid
on 25 mm mortar bed

precast concrete
kerb laid on
15-25 mm mortar
bed haunched
both sides

100 mm well consolidated
base

100 - 150

150

375 min

● subgrade imported or approved existing soil

Figure 4.3   Precast concrete kerb detail in rigid paving finished with brick pavers.

should be laid out in panels of not more than 10m², with the greatest dimension not more than 4.5m–6.0m, surrounded by movement joints. A movement joint should also be incorporated into the concrete slab below. There are a variety of fillers for movement joints, compressible foam-type material, pointed with a tack-free polysulphide sealant at the surface, being frequently used.

The best type of pointing to express the joints and yet avoid excessive standing water, which in turn leads to deterioration caused by cycles of freeze-thaw conditions, is a bucket handle joint. On paved surfaces, particularly in constant shade, recessed joints encourage slippery moss and lichen growth which may cause accidents. Nonetheless, mossy joints can be visually pleasing and acceptable in a domestic setting. To encourage mosses, the recessed joints may be filled with a mixture of sand and topsoil.

Drainage falls

Adequate gradients are essential to drain both rigid and flexible brick paving. In stretcher-bond paving, the direction of the fall should follow the main joint lines. Gradients for both rigid and flexible brick paving should not be less than 1:60, 1:40 being preferred. Brick drainage channels, with a minimum longitudinal fall of about 1:80, can be incorporated into the paving design to maximize the dry walking area.

Design

In designing with brick, it is especially important that the overall concept is developed and applied in a unified fashion. The way the individual units meet, the paving patterns, the edge details, the junctions with other materials should all be carefully considered. Cecil Handisyde in *Hard Landscape in Brick* suggests a five-point critical design approach:

1. Does the chosen unit face size give the scale required, or should a second scale be superimposed?
2. Will a proposed pattern involve special units or an unacceptable amount of cutting? Note that the edge cutting becomes relatively less important as areas increase.
3. Is a directional pattern required to emphasize a particular route, to provide

maximum joint grip, or to improve water run-off from minimum fall areas?

4. Is a good interlocking pattern required to prevent lateral displacement (as in vehicular areas)?

5. Is advantage to be taken of the considerable differences in appearance that result from units of different exposed face size, shape or colour being used for basically similar patterns?

In rigid paving, bricks can be laid on their bed face or on edge. On the bed face, the proportion of length to width is 2:1 whereas, when laid on edge, a brick gives a proportion of 3:1. Pavers less than 65mm thick are not normally considered suitable for laying on edge.

The most common brick paving patterns are as follows:

Running or stretcher bond

This runs either with the direction of traffic or across it. In the former, long joint lines are apparent and an accurately set-out edge restraint is essential to prevent the lines of pavers from wavering. Quarter, half and third lap bond can be used to accentuate the pattern. When laid as flexible paving, stretcher bond is sufficiently effective in locking the brick courses for pedestrian use, but is not the most suitable for vehicle use.

Herringbone

This gives the best paver interlock in flexible paving and creates a consistent pattern viewed from any direction. Normally it is laid at 45° to the edge of the paving, to minimize the visual effects of misalignment. Use of the triangular edging specials produced by some brick manufacturers avoids the expense of edge-cutting. Herringbone can also be laid at 90° to the edge. It is best to frame the herringbone area with a soldier course or a specially designed edging block. Herringbone is the most suitable bond in flexible paving patterns for vehicular use.

Basketweave

Basketweave has several variations based on a proportion of 3:1 or 2:1. Large areas may be subdivided into bays by bands of contrasting bricks, within which basketweave paving is laid. As there are long, unbonded joints, it is not suitable for vehicular areas unless rigid construction is adopted. Like stack bond, some sorting may be necessary with bricks of inconsistent size to achieve a good appearance. This is a difficult bond to lay satisfactorily as flexible paving.

Stack bond

Also known as grid pattern, stack bond is decorative and can be charming in small areas such as courtyards and small enclosed gardens where it echoes the geometric form of buildings. As it has poor interlock, because of the continuous joint in two directions, it should be restricted to rigid construction.

Circular or curved patterns

These can be created with bricks because of their small unit size, using half bricks, brick-on-edge or brick-on-end. A rigid construction is essential for

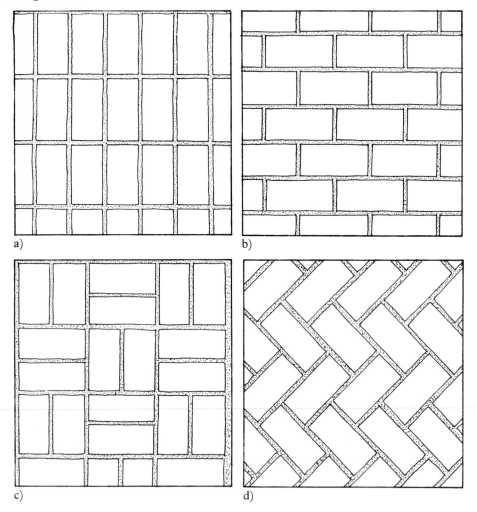

Figure 4.4   Brick paving patterns and bonds; a) stack, b) stretcher, c) basketweave, d) herringbone.

smaller radii. The construction of circular patterns requires a high degree of skill to obtain joints which are neither too wide nor too narrow. It is most attractive when well done.

Jointing

Jointing can emphasize a design if coloured mortar is used, but mortar colours do fade and are vulnerable to dirt and staining. It is desirable to lay sample panels of brick and mortar colour combinations before finalizing mortar colours.

Scale

An increase in pattern scale can be achieved by superimposing bands or grids of contrasting brick within the overall pattern, as already suggested for natural stone pavings. In addition to colour differences, subtle textural changes or use of other materials, such as cobbles or natural stone, can achieve a similarly attractive effect.

Steps in Brick

Frost-resistant bricks can be used to build the treads, risers and walls on each side where these are necessary. Nosings or wall copings may be differentiated by colour. Conversely, by using the same type of brick, steps can extend the character of a building out into its immediate setting.

The bricks must be firmly bedded and mortar jointed. Where it may be necessary to take trolleys down steps, bullnosed bricks should be used to form a rounded leading edge and so minimize damage. Particularly heavy use may suggest an alternative material such as a hard stone or concrete. Projecting the tread slightly, some 25mm over the riser, produces a shadow line, which helps to emphasize each step. A combination of brick risers with stone or precast concrete treads has the advantage of allowing for a thinner tread. The colour combination may, however, prove too disturbing.

It is, of course, potentially dangerous to use smooth materials for outdoor steps so a surface texture should be considered when selecting bricks or pavers. Amongst the most slip-resistant are the patterned engineering bricks, such as stable pavers.

Where pavers are laid onto preformed concrete steps, a brushed bitumen damp-proof membrane, dressed with sharp sand, should be applied to the concrete surface to minimize the risk of lime from the concrete being leached out by groundwater and staining the brickwork.

Figure 4.5   Interesting use of brick paving to form a pedestrian ramp.

Clay Tiles

Mediterranean countries provide many good example of glazed and unglazed clay tiles used to striking effect in urban squares and domestic courtyards. However, in Britain only semi-vitrified tiles of external quality can be used, because of the possibility of frost damage. Clay tiles should have low water absorption qualities, and the manufacturer's advice on their frost resistance should be sought in relation to BS 6431: pt22: 1986.

Characteristics

Quarry and semi-vitrified external tiles range in plan sizes between 225 x 225mm and 100 x 100mm, with a thickness of 12–30mm. Quarry tiles are made from natural clay which has been plasticized and well burnt. They are usually square or rectangular but are also available in special forms, such as hexagons. Semi-vitrified tiles are prepared from refined clay which can be coloured and textured before firing.

Construction

Tiles must be mortar bedded on an accurately levelled concrete base. The prospect of tiles working loose – a frequent cause of failure – has been much reduced by manufacturing them with a dovetail key on the base to give a positive mechanical bond with the mortar bed. Expansion joints in the supporting concrete slabs must be carried through to the surface of the tiles. To prevent puddles forming, and to minimize frost damage, tile paving should be laid to adequate falls. Well-maintained joints are also important to exclude water from the mortar bed in order to avoid frost heave.

Design

Whilst tiles are more expensive than either brick pavers or concrete block paving, they do have considerable potential. In the design of the entrance areas to buildings, for example, they can help to relate internal and external spaces because they are appropriate to both locations.

Figure 4.6   Corner detail of a flight of steps.

Figure 4.7   Neat brick steps can blend into informal garden design.

Figure 4.8   Converging planes of brick paviors cleverly used to negotiate awkward changes in level.

CHAPTER 5

Concrete

Precast Paving Slabs

Traditionally laid at the scale and in the style of stone flags, precast concrete paving slabs have now widely replaced natural stone, except in civic schemes or where the predominant existing paving material is natural stone. The majority of paving slabs are produced by the wet-pressing or dry-pressing method. These techniques are used for the mass-production of high-quality products.

Characteristics

All square or rectangular paving slabs made to BS 368 are to standardized sizes, acceptable levels of strength and frost resistance. The most common plan sizes are 900 x 600mm, 600 x 600mm, either 63mm or 50mm thick. Manufacturers make BS sizes, which helps in matching new work with old and allows supplies from different manufacturers to be mixed, as well as non-standard sizes.

Because vehicles driven over footways frequently break paving slabs, on roadside pavements smaller slabs are now becoming more widely used instead of the traditional 900 x 600mm. These can carry five-tonne wheel loads and are manufactured in four sizes; 300 x 300 x 60mm, 400 x 400 x 65mm, 450 x 450 x 70mm and 450 x 450 x 100mm. For non-traffic areas, they are available 50mm thick in all these sizes.

A variety of slab shapes, such as hexagons and circles, are produced but are not now commonly used except as stepping stones. The colour of the ordinary Portland cement used in standard slabs results in shades of grey, but various colours can be introduced through the use of aggregates or pigments. Red, black, brown or white aggregates can be incorporated into the mix and, using secondary processing, a variety of features can be achieved. These aggregate colours are both subtle and permanent. Subtlety is not a characteristic of pigmented slabs which are, at first, unnatural shades of green, red or buff, and then fade within a few years and look grubby. The neutral, light and dark grey tones of precast paving should be valued for their own intrinsic qualities. Used skilfully, they form an effective foil to the colours of planting, landscape furniture and buildings.

Some manufacturers produce a wide range of textured slabs including patterned by moulding (for example, raised chequers, dimples, grooves or ribs), by incorporating rubber inserts, shot blasting the surface or exposing the aggregate. Material such as calcined bauxite can also be added to the surface, to reduce slipperiness.

Slabs with raised dots are produced specifically for the partially sighted or

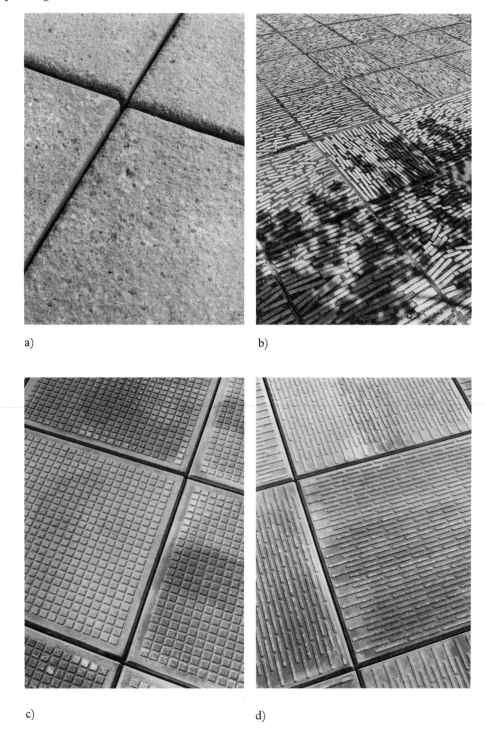

a)   b)

c)   d)

Figure 5.1   A wide range of textured, precast paving slabs is available; a) a shot blasted finish reveals the stone aggregate, b) inlaid concrete fragments create a striking pattern, c) and d) textured moulds produce anti-slip surfaces.

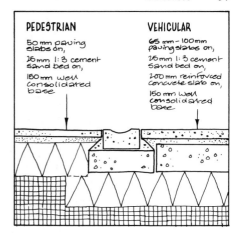

PEDESTRIAN

50mm paving slabs on,

25mm 1:3 cement sand bed on,

150mm well consolidated base

VEHICULAR

65mm–100mm paving slabs on,

25mm 1:3 cement sand bed on,

200mm reinforced concrete slab on,

150mm well consolidated base

Figure 5.2 Multi-section showing pavement construction using different thickness precast concrete slabs for pedestrian and light vehicular use.

blind, who can immediately identify a danger zone, such as a crossing, without the paving being dangerous for other pedestrians. It is not comfortable to walk on, however.

Construction

For pedestrian use in public areas, precast concrete slabs should be laid on a 25mm thick bed of lime:sand mortar (1:3 to 1:4) or cement:sand mortar (1:3 to 1:4), supported by a well consolidated base of at least 100mm. A lime:sand bed facilitates cleaning of slabs, where lifting and relaying are anticipated and a cement:sand bed is stronger where occasional light vehicular traffic may occur.

Where heavy vehicle traffic is anticipated – for example at pavement crossings or areas for vehicular use – the smaller slabs mentioned above should be used, supported by a suitable base.

In private gardens, precast concrete slabs may be laid on a bed of coarse sand, again supported by a well consolidated base. They are levelled and secured in place by a generous trowel-full of lime mortar placed near each corner and in the centre.

The minimum effective fall to remove surface water from precast slabs is 1:70 but this can be increased to 1:40 to improve run-off over large areas.

On slopes steeper than about 1:15, textured finishes are desirable to reduce accidents, especially in wet weather.

Drainage is most reliably achieved by falls to gullies and channels at regular intervals. As falls in two directions result in unattractive, diagonal cutting of slabs, it is better to design the paving with a single fall to drainage channels which take up the longitudinal fall internally as shown in the diagram. Channels and gullies should be laid to follow the bond line of the slabs. These drainage units are available in sizes which integrate with standard slab sizes.

Slabs may be laid with the joints close-jointed, mortar-filled or open. Close joints are best filled with sand. If sand:cement mortar is used, staining may occur. Wider joints, 6mm–12mm wide, should be pointed. Suitable mortar mixes for pointing are cement:lime:sand (1:1/4:3 to 1:1/2:4), cement:sand 1:4 or masonry cement:sand 1:2 to 1:3. Again, care is needed in pointing, as excess mortar leaves a stain if it is not removed immediately. Stain removal is particularly difficult with textured slabs.

As with brick walling, the type of pointing can accentuate or play down the importance of the junction between units. A smooth-finished bucket handle joint

Figure 5.3 *Top:*   Manipulation of bonding patterns can enhance the character of slab paving.

Figure 5.4 *Right:*   Smaller concrete paving slabs on a suitable base can be used in areas of heavy traffic loading.

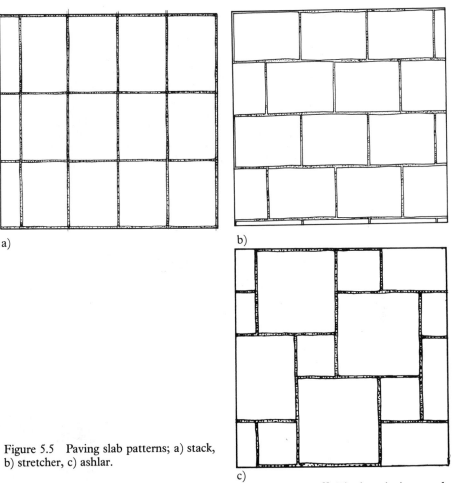

a)

b)

Figure 5.5   Paving slab patterns; a) stack,
b) stretcher, c) ashlar.

c)

performs most satisfactorily, encouraging water to run off. Flush pointing tends
to spread out from the joint over adjacent slabs and so may look untidy unless
carried out with very considerable skill. If a raked-out joint is used, accumulated
water tends to freeze in winter, leading to the breakdown of the mortar and
accumulation of grit and weeds in the joints.

Open joints, say 50–150mm wide, can be effective in reducing the visual
impact or formality of a paved area, or in suggesting priority of direction. The
gaps between the slabs can be filled with other paving materials, such as brick,
setts or loose material such as gravel, depending on the intensity of use, to
create a sympathetic and perhaps contrasting finish. Similarly, where foot traffic
is very light, low, tough ground-cover plants can be used to create an attractive
division between areas of paving.

A gap between slabs wider than 150mm suggests informal stepping stones.
The distance between the centres of these slabs should coincide with the normal
walking pace. If used in association with grass, it is important to set the slabs
low enough to allow normal mowing to be carried out.

Design

Precast concrete slabs are a relatively low-cost way of providing paving. The
quality and atmosphere of a particular location can be enhanced by the selection

of an appropriate slab and kerb or other edge trim. Its character can be further developed by manipulating the bonding, sizes, colour, texture and joint detailing and by skilful design of levels, falls and edges.

Too many slabs cut to awkward shapes give an untidy appearance and suggest that the scheme has been ill-considered. Cutting can be minimized by basing the setting-out of the design on multiples of slab sizes or by introducing smaller units at the margins of the paved area.

The usual bonds are stretcher bond and stack bond. Flemish bond also forms a large paving module with two units – one square and one rectangular.

Hexagonal or octagonal slabs create a non-directional, bonded pattern. To avoid cutting or awkward junctions, they are best used where they adjoin, say, low planting without a raised kerb. The range is more restricted in size and finish than in rectangular slabs.

Circular slabs can be used to form stepping stones, set into planting, grass, gravel or cobbles.

Composite patterns are now possible, using units manufactured in complementary octagons and squares. These can appear too fussy for large areas of paving, but can give a special character to small spaces.

Special Units

A number of products are made from precast concrete for special situations, such as erosion control, tree surrounds and step units.

Figure 5.6   When laid on a correctly designed base, concrete block paving will withstand high point loads, such as aircraft wheels.

Figure 5.7 Special precast concrete
paving units can reinforce grass areas
subjected to occasional vehicle traffic.

Erosion control

Where occasional vehicle access is required onto grassed areas, such as car
parking at rural parks or showgrounds, overflow parking areas or fire access
routes, the ground surface can be reinforced with lattice-like concrete units,
which allow grass to grow in the openings.

The establishment of grass is obtained by laying the concrete units onto a
sand bed over a layer of quarry waste or similar material. This base should
contain fine material, or loam from which the grass roots can draw
nourishment. The interstices are filled with good quality topsoil to some 30mm
below the top surface. A seed mix of resilient grasses is distributed evenly and
covered with topsoil to finish 20mm below the top surface to prevent vehicles
damaging the grass.

Reinforced grass is more appropriate than *in situ* concrete or blacktop in
many situations, making the necessary careful maintenance worthwhile.

Concrete Block Paving

Although only introduced to Britain over the past few decades, precast concrete
unit 'flexible' paving has been used in continental Europe for much longer.
Being both visually satisfying and potentially strong, it has a wide range of
applications.

When laid on a correctly designed base, concrete block paving will withstand
high point loads like the wheels of trailers or small jockey wheels. Their major
advantage over *in situ* materials is that they can easily be lifted and replaced
with comparatively little evidence of disturbance.

Characteristics

Precast concrete paving blocks are manufactured to BS 6717, Part 1 (1986)
'Specification for paving blocks'. They are similar to paving bricks in size,
rectangular blocks having an upper face of approximately 100 x 200mm. A

number of more complex, and more expensive, interlocking shapes are made to similar dimensions. Blocks are manufactured in a range of thicknesses, to suit different loadings for example, 65mm thick for pedestrian areas and 80–100mm for heavy-duty applications.

The majority of blocks are produced with chamfered edges, although some manufacturers produce blocks with pencil round edges to provide a more uniform ride for small-wheeled vehicles such as supermarket trolleys.

Concrete paving blocks are available in a range of colours, from pale grey and buff, through reds and browns to almost black. As well as uniform colouring, some mottled effects have been developed to suggest the random pattern found in brindled bricks. Some variation in pigmentation may occur, so care should be taken in colour-matching when different batches are used for a large area of paving. One should be aware that, in time, the leaching out of pigments reduces the intensity of colour and contrasts achieved in the original design.

For car or heavy vehicle parking areas, concrete block paving is ideal as it is not structurally affected by oil spillage (unlike bitumen macadam paving). However, stains are very apparent on light-coloured units, although less so on dark grey or brown ones.

Simulated stone setts are also produced from concrete, in a range of shapes and sizes, enabling them to be laid to traditional patterns such as the fan, but they lack the varied character of natural stone setts.

Construction

The method of laying concrete block paving to form a flexible pavement is much the same as that used for brick. Crucial to the pavement's success is the construction of an appropriate base course. The type, weight, speed and numbers of vehicles using the surface during its design life must be taken into account, along with the load-bearing capacity of the subsoil. (See 'Road Note 29' DTP, 1979). The base thickness should be a minimum of 150mm for lightly trafficked roads such as cul-de-sacs and 100mm for pedestrian areas.

Over the base is spread a bed of sand on to which the paving blocks are laid. The blocks are then vibrated. The final thickness of the sand bed is 50mm.

A close-butted joint is necessary to achieve interlock between adjacent blocks,

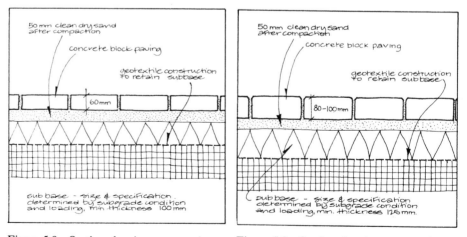

Figure 5.8   Section showing construction of 60mm thick precast concrete block paving for pedestrian use.

Figure 5.9   Section showing construction of 80–100mm thick precast concrete block paving for vehicular use.

Figure 5.10 Simulated stone setts are produced that can emulate traditional sett patterns like the fan, but they lack the varied character of natural stone.

which are then able to spread loads evenly over what becomes, in effect, a single flexible pavement. This is achieved by the use of joints not more than 4mm wide, filled with sand to BS 882, Class C. The sand is spread over the whole surface and the blocks are vibrated again. Then the sand is topped up, before a final vibration. All these operations should be planned so that all the work is completed on a daily basis. On some products, projecting spacers are cast on to the sides to ensure that the joint is of the correct width.

Edge restraint is essential. Without structurally rigid edges on all sides of a paved area, continuity of surface and horizontal transmission of load cannot be obtained and the blocks would then become loose. The edge restraint can take the form of matching kerb units or channels or a soldier course of the same block set in mortar on a concrete foundation with hidden haunching. This allows a harmonious continuity of the pavement over the whole surface. Standard concrete kerbs (BS 340) can be used to create a solid, more clearly visible edge treatment, but care is needed to ensure that they relate well to the smaller scale and different colour of the paving blocks.

After a concrete block pavement has been in use for a while, the joints become sealed by fine silt or dust and the surface is virtually impermeable, so longitudinal falls should be a minimum of 1:80 and crossfalls at least 1:40. Further advice on construction techniques is available from Interpave, the Concrete Block Paving Association, or from manufacturers.

Figure 5.11 *Above:*   The incorporation of an edge constraint is essential when designing a concrete block pavement.

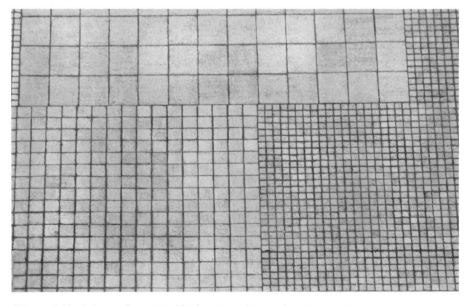

Figure 5.12 *Below:*   Concrete block proportions selected to allow innovative paving design.

Figure 5.13 The range of precast sett sizes available allows considerable design flexibility.

Design

The patterns that can be achieved with rectangular concrete blocks are those derived from the brick paving traditions as described on page 49. Stretcher bond, herringbone and basketweave are the most common and satisfactory forms. Where herringbone pattern is laid at 45° to the kerb, special triangular edging units known as 'Bishop's hats' can be used, to avoid cutting. Herringbone pattern laid at 90° to the kerb and stretcher-bond needs little cutting since half blocks are available. But, where cut blocks are unavoidable, they should not be less than one-third the length of a full block.

For vehicular use, rectangular blocks must be laid to a herringbone pattern, to give the necessary degree of bonding. It is generally accepted that there is no greater interlock benefit from the more complicated and more expensive shapes available.

Markings, such as the lines used to define parking bays, can be incorporated into a pattern, using different coloured or specially produced blocks.

Figure 5.14 *Top:*   In-situ concrete can be attractive if skilfully designed and laid.

Figure 5.15 *Bottom:*   Larger concrete modules can be successfully used in informal garden design.

In Situ **Concrete**

In situ concrete makes a good, low-cost paving that can be attractive if skilfully designed and laid. The materials are readily available, and it is relatively straightforward to lay in large or small areas, with few limitations on shapes or falls. These very qualities have sometimes resulted in the material being held in low esteem. *In situ* concrete may sometimes be unkempt, cracked and stained, but this need not be so if care is taken to assess the proposed use and to specify an appropriate construction and finishing technique for the particular conditions. It is appropriate for a wide range of situations, from paths to retaining walls.

Finishing techniques

The surface of *in situ* concrete can be enriched by applying aggregate or by exposing the aggregate used in the mix. There is a wide range of aggregates, varying in size, shape and colour. Alternatively, a number of methods are available for impressing a pattern into the surface.

Construction

The load-bearing capacity of *in situ* concrete depends on the construction of the base course and the thickness of the concrete slab itself which can vary from a minimum of 75mm to as much as 300mm. The supporting base course must always be well consolidated on an adequate 'formation' – that is, a properly drained and consolidated sub soil or rock. Since concrete shrinks on setting, and is also subject to some seasonal shrinkage and expansion, movement joints are necessary. This restricts the bay size to 10m² (maximum 4.0m in any direction) in unreinforced concrete.

Joints between bays are normally formed by battens, inserted to one-third of the depth of the concrete, which are removed before the concrete sets. The joint, about 15mm wide, is filled with compressible joint filler and topped with a firm but flexible sealant. Alternatively, the joint can be clearly expressed using another material, such as a row of setts to make a contrast with the concrete. Cracking is thus controlled, because it tends to occur at the junction between the two materials.

To resist cracking, a light mesh of steel reinforcement is normally

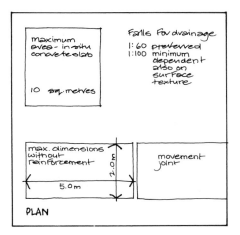

Figure 5.16 In-situ concrete bay dimensions showing area, falls and reinforcement requirements.

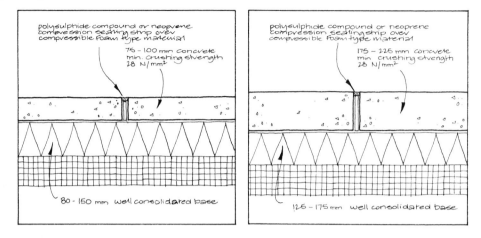

Figure 5.17   In-situ concrete paving constructed for; a) pedestrian use, b) light vehicular loading.

incorporated in larger bays. This serves to spread loadings and is particularly necessary on made-up ground.

To ensure effective drainage of an *in situ* concrete surface, an optimum gradient of 1:60 should be used, although for small areas of paving, gradients of up to 1:12 can be considered. Textural quality affects drainage performance, so coarser surfaces require steeper gradients.

To form an exposed aggregate finish, the aggregate is tamped in until it has disappeared below the wet cement and the panel is then left for a short time, the length of time depending on the concrete mix and the temperature-dependent rate of concrete curing or hardening. The use of retardent admixtures on the concrete surface can assist in the process of exposing aggregates. The aggregate is then exposed by brushing the surface under a fine spray of water. Other methods of exposure include abrasive blasting and high-pressure water-jetting.

Tamping regular grooves across a panel of concrete with a timber board creates a slip-resistant surface, as well as alleviating the blandness of smooth concrete. Alternatively, to create a finer, softer-looking texture, a brushed finish may be achieved by pulling a stiff brush across the concrete as it sets.

There are several machines available for forming indented patterns. These can be used in a purely repetitive way, or, like any other machine-aided operation, be carried out to a creative design by a skilled and sympathetic worker. They include indented rings, grids and simulated setts.

There are also proprietary systems available for casting special concrete finishes, such as *in situ* grass-reinforcement. The concrete is cast into polystyrene moulds, which are burnt away when it has set. However, the ensuing air pollution caused by this operation must now render these types of finish undesirable.

The surface appearance of *in situ* concrete can be united with its surroundings in terms of texture, colour or scale, and also through judicious choice of aggregate, colour or pattern. The use of another material, such as brick, for movement joints can also be used to create a visual link with buildings or walls.

Both the appearance and the future use of the pavement must be carefully considered when selecting the surface treatment: for example, sharp aggregates should not be used where children may play.

Inspection covers are essential to provide access to underground services beneath *in situ* concrete, because it is virtually impossible to re-lay and match. In new developments, services routes should, if possible, avoid *in situ* paving. They are better placed below grass or gravel where access is easier and where repairs carried out with care will be inconspicuous.

Figure 5.18 *Right:*   In-situ concrete paving has the great advantage that it can be laid to flowing shapes.

Figure 5.19 *Below:*   Where in-situ concrete is used with another material, such as brick, it can create a visual link with surrounding buildings.

CHAPTER 6

Asphalt and bound surfaces

This chapter covers asphalts (that is, hot-rolled and mastic asphalt), and coated macadams, (that is, tarmacadam, bitumen macadam and cold asphalt which is, in fact, a form of macadam). They are the most widely applied of all paved surfaces, being suitable in one form or another for many situations, from intensive, heavy vehicle traffic to light pedestrian use. Generally cheap, compared to unit paving, they are flexible, reasonably durable and easy to handle, although there are some drawbacks. In fact, their very versatility results in underuse of appropriate alternatives. Although lower in initial cost than unit paving, this may be offset by heavier maintenance requirements in later years, so the key consideration should be their annual cost-in-use.

Characteristics

To understand their design potential and application, it is necessary to look first at the various flexible bound surfaces available and their durability.

The suggested working lives stated below assume no maintenance because this is largely an undetermined variable. The life of macadam surfaces may be extended by the application of a surface seal, such as tar or bitumen spray with chippings.

Hot-rolled asphalt (BS 594)

This is composed of a bitumen binder and gap-graded aggregate – that is, a mixture of sand and coarse aggregate, without medium-sized particles. It is virtually impermeable and its smooth and relatively slippery surface is textured for skid-resistance by rolling coating chippings into it, which should be as uniform in size as possible, to ensure that the binder coats the aggregate evenly and that the chippings can be satisfactorily spread and embedded into the asphalt. Hot-rolled asphalt, the highest-quality surfacing used on public roadways, is comparatively expensive. Nevertheless, it is very durable under heavy trafficking and has a life of between fifteen and twenty years.

Mastic asphalt (BS 1447)

This asphalt has the highest bitumen content of all and is therefore the most expensive flexible surfacing. It is used in special situations where traffic is heavy, for example in loading bays or bus laybys and on rooftop car parks. Mastic asphalt does not easily deteriorate if laid upon a well compacted and sound base and may last up to twenty years. Spreading is carried out by hand and the finish is very smooth, so bitumen-coated chippings are usually rolled into the surface to improve the skid-resistance on roads. On pedestrian areas, mastic asphalt usually has a sand-rubbed finish.

Bitumen macadam (BS 4987)

This is a bitumen-coated stone mixture which is rolled until the stone particles interlock. Some mixtures can be quite porous in the early years but dense, and reasonably impervious, varieties of macadam are also available. Bituminous macadam is unsuitable for surfaces where appreciable quantities of oil or petrol may be spilled. Coloured finishes are available, but they add significantly to the cost, compared with basic macadam. The life of bitumen macadam is in the order of seven to eight years, but this can be extended by applying a surface dressing of tar or bitumen spray with chippings.

Tarmacadam (BS 4987)

Tarmacadam is no longer generally available, since it was made using the tar obtained as a by-product of gas extraction from coal. The limited amount of tar produced from the processing of smokeless coal is used for road surface dressing treatments or the manufacture of dense tar surfacing. Dense tar surfacing is resistant to softening by oil products, so has a specialized use where abnormal spillage is anticipated.

Cold asphalt (BS 4987)

This is a fine, bitumen-coated aggregate material, often used to cover or repair existing bituminous surfaces in lightly used areas.

The quality of construction, the intensity of use of the pavement and the promptness of repair are all influences on the durability of bitumen-bound and asphalt surfaces. The texture of the surface is influenced by the proportions of firm aggregate used within the flexible bound material and, in the case of rolled asphalt and cold asphalt, by rolling in coated chippings.

Construction

The construction of public highways falls outside the scope of this Guide and reference should be made to the Department of Transport's 'Specification for Road and Bridge Works' for further information on this topic.

All of these bound materials are laid on a thoroughly compacted base and sub-base. The thickness of the course and the selection of the aggregate size is dependent on the ground conditions and future use. The sub-base should be well drained in all cases. The thickness of the surfacing is usually approximately 60mm for pedestrian and light vehicular use. This may consist of a single layer of a relatively coarse material, such as single-course macadam or of two courses – for example, a 20mm surface layer of a finer material, such as cold asphalt, on top of a 40mm base course of coated macadam. Thicker layers of stronger materials, such as dense macadam or hot rolled asphalt, are necessary for heavy usage.

The bound materials are compacted by rolling, using a minimum roller weight of 2.5 tonnes (6–10 tonnes for roads), although a hand roller may be necessary for narrow or awkward areas. A firm edge restraint is necessary around all margins, to prevent the material spreading or crumbling during this operation. This is usually provided by concrete or brick kerbs haunched on concrete foundations. Small precast concrete edging, measuring 50 x 205mm on section, 'heel kerbs', are only suitable for footpaths, as they soon work loose under vehicle loading, leading to outward creep and deterioration of the bound surface.

Standing water in or on bound surfaces is always a potential hazard because of stresses caused by alternate freezing and thawing. There are two aspects to the provision of adequate drainage necessary to limit the potential for damage.

1. Water build-up in the lower layers must be prevented by controlling ingress at the sides and from the surface.
2. Ponding on impervious surfaces must be prevented by the provision of adequate surface water drainage falls.

Generally macadams are best laid to a minimum fall of 1:40 and asphalts to 1:50. Where level or near-level surfaces are required, then asphalt should be used, with the whole construction laid to *very* accurate levels on an evenly consolidated base to avoid the shallowest depressions.

Design

The dull, dark tone of fine cold asphalt can be relieved by rolling in a scattering of white or red stone chippings. Uncoated chippings are not suitable for the other forms of bitumen surfacing. Another means of improving the relatively dull visual character of 'blacktop' is to use unit paving materials such as stone setts or bricks laid in the form of a 'framework' or edging. The risk of damaging them when rolling the blacktop should be recognized and consideration should be given to providing temporary protection against roller damage.

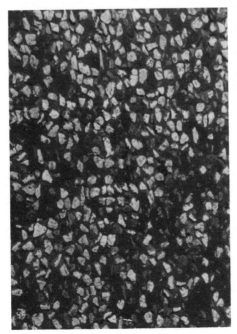

Figure 6.1 *Left:* A dark bound surface can be made more attractive if a scattering of light stone chippings is rolled into the surface.

Figure 6.2 *Below:* Edging detail to macadam pavement.

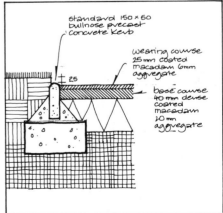

CHAPTER 7

Timber

Timber has a natural affinity with vegetation, making it an attractive material for landscape work in general. It can be used at a range of scales, from massive bridge timbers to small paving blocks. The texture may be rough or smooth. The great range of available timbers offers designers a wide choice but, as most timbers are liable to decay in contact with the soil, its use as paving must be approached with caution.

Timbers decay at different rates under the same conditions. The Timber Research and Development Association has grouped timbers into five categories, according to their durability in ground contact, ranging from 'perishable' (less than five years) to 'very durable' (more than twenty-five years). These can be referred to in TRADA's Wood Information Sheet 'Timbers – Their Properties and Uses'. The life expectancy of many perishable timbers can be extended by treatment with preservatives, which are described in the TRADA Wood Information Sheet 'Preservative Treatment for Timber – A Guide to Specification'. Timbers that may be used generally without treatment include sweet chestnut, oak, larch, western red cedar and the imported greenheart.

A range of durable but expensive hardwoods, such as ekki and iroko, from tropical and semi-tropical forests is available. Although very durable, scarcity through the regrettable exploitation of tropical rain forests may soon make them practically unobtainable. It is clearly desirable to find more economic alternatives to ensure that such finite natural resources are not exploited. Each timber has its own natural colour. Moreover, there are now many stains which have been developed specifically for external use and which offer variable degrees of protection, as well as an exciting range of colours.

Texture can be emphasized by selection of different types of grain and by cutting techniques. It may be rough-hewn with an axe or adze, cut with a coarse cross-cut saw when green, or with a mechanical band saw or, at the other end of the scale, with a fine tenon saw. It may be left 'as sawn', or planed smooth. Timber logs are more likely to be suitable for rural situations, whereas the crispness of sawn or planed timber fits in better with the built environment.

Construction

Since timber decays fastest at the zone just below the surface of the soil where the soil micro-organisms, moisture and air are all present, detailing of timber structures or decking must take account of this to achieve an economic life. For example:

Figure 7.1   Timber decking provides an excellent waterside surface for recreational activities.

Figure 7.2   Rough hewn timber is ideal for step risers on gravel paths.

- Contact with the ground should be limited by using metal bases for posts or by using substructures of more durable timbers or precast concrete posts and framing.
- A bed of coarse aggregate should be provided below ground-level to ensure free drainage. For example, treated timber railway sleepers, resting on well drained ballast, have lasted for many years.
- Where possible, some protection from the elements, such as a covered way over a board walk, should be provided.

Design

Timber can be used externally in a wide range of situations. Outdoor decks can be constructed in timber to extend indoor spaces. Permanent raised boardwalks are ideal for visitor access over marshy land in places such as nature reserves. The open slats allow free drainage of rainwater from the surface. Strong temporary paths over rough ground, unstable sand or dunes can be formed by wiring planks together. They are both easy to lay and to roll up and remove. If made of durable wood, like hornbeam or chestnut, they may be re-usable.

At one time, timber setts in a tar matrix were used for roadways, but timber blocks at ground level do become very slippery and are really only suitable for private or semi-private use. However, log cross-sections set into the ground, with the gaps filled with gravel or similar porous materials, form an attractive garden surface. Large diameter sections can be used as 'stepping stones'.

Timber has traditionally been used to build small-span bridges. For spans up to, say, three metres the simple beam form is ideal. Longer-span bridges can be constructed using laminated and stress-graded timber, which can be more elegant than steel and concrete, with similar beam depth-span ratios. There are a number of manufacturers who specialize in prefabricated timber bridges.

Timber can be used in combination with other paving materials, for instance to form simple risers on flights of outdoor steps, or stepped ramps retaining a porous gravel tread for good drainage. As the riser must form a firm nosing for safety reasons, it should be at least 50mm thick and should be anchored securely into the ground with rigid metal or stout timber pegs. In rural areas, riven logs can be used in this way most attractively. Where there is a change of level on an informal path, timber risers are ideal. They can easily be adjusted to suit a variable width of path or height of riser, giving maximum flexibility.

Figure 7.3   Cross-sections of tree trunk make delightful stepping stones for an informal garden path, though they become slippery in time if not cleaned.

CHAPTER 8

Safer Surfaces for use with Play Equipment

The overall design of play spaces is a specialist subject outside the scope of this volume. However, the use of shock-absorbent surfaces beneath play equipment is an essential feature of play provision and paving design and so is included here.

It is essential that all playground equipment is robust in manufacture with secure joints, hidden, or otherwise unobtrusive, fastenings and secure ground mountings. To avoid serious injuries, the 'fall height' from platforms should be *less* than 2.50m above adjoining ground levels. All equipment should be at least as good as the latest edition of the related British Standard (BS 5696) and be maintained to that standard at all times through regular professional inspection.

Play equipment should always be associated with an underlying carpet of impact-absorbent materials.

Natural Shock-Absorbent Surfaces

Wherever there is a danger of children falling off equipment, the landing surface should cushion that fall. The danger is increased when children are in motion above the ground. It is unwise to specify or indeed accept, rigid, unyielding paving materials, such as concrete or tarmac, beneath play apparatus in view of the obvious risk to children. Hard soil even with a grass covering is not acceptable either as it may well contain large or sharp stones.

Elsewhere in Europe play spaces with large area of sand are successfully used, but in most of Britain the difficulties of educating the general public to prevent the introduction of broken glass or fouling by pet animals has, unfortunately, largely prevented its adoption. Sand is an exciting and safe medium for children, given good management: this includes responsible parental supervision, a daily raking-over of the surface, good drainage, dog-excluding fences with self-closing gates and a willingness to replace the sand annually. A conflict of use arises if the areas of sand are too small and young children are attracted to landing areas beneath apparatus because there is no general sand play-zone.

Other shock-absorbent surfaces which can be considered are pea shingle and tree bark, a by-product of the timber industry, but these materials require even more management than sand to prevent them being dispersed and because they can also hide broken glass. Some barks support slow combustion and also gradually decompose, so they need more frequent replacement.

Artificial Shock-Absorbent Surfaces

Where management cannot provide daily raking and supervision, rubber-based shock absorbent materials are a better alternative to either sand or shredded bark immediately around and under above-ground play equipment. These are based on rubber crumbs held together by binding agents and expanded by various inert fillers before being made into slabs, rolls or material to be laid *in situ*.

A series of tests carried out by the Department of the Environment some years ago showed that the best materials were nearly as good as clean dry sand, but the worst were quite unsatisfactory in that they appeared to be resilient at first sight but were little better than tarmac when tested electronically in the laboratory.

There are now many good products on the market which meet the criteria laid down in the British Standard 5696 for limiting the acceleration of a falling child on initial contact with the ground surface, from a height not exceeding 2.50m, to a tolerably safe level. The best of them decelerate the child's body by a resilient surface supported by ribs of the same material which then deform under load to further reduce the final speed, and thus the force, of the impact. However, a specifier must be satisfied with the proven and tested qualities of any artificial shock-absorbent surface before selecting a particular product.

Figure 8.1   Tree bark is becoming popular as a natural shock-absorbent surface.

PART II

Enclosures

CHAPTER 9

Enclosures

Before deciding on the form and extent of landscape enclosure, the precise functional and aesthetic requirements of the design brief should be precisely defined. Enclosure in landscape, as the illustrations show, must be considered in conjunction with the other elements in the design.

Before considering the form of an enclosure, it is essential to consider the space which is to be created: 'To have significant spaces you must have enclosure, and the size, shape and character of the enclosure determines the quality of the space. Openness, void or mere expanse are not enough; they may be only emptiness.'[1]

Perception of outdoor space is conditioned by personal experience. If the form and scale of a space does not suit its apparent function, a sense of dissatisfaction can be experienced. For example, an area labelled 'children's play' in the corner of a large field, without any kind of enclosure, lacks child appeal and could well remain unused. Interestingly, the same volume of space can appear to be quite different in an urban, compared with a rural, setting.

The proportions of surrounding or enclosing elements greatly influence the way in which space is perceived, whatever the scale. When the 'walls' are very low in relation to the space they contain, the space enclosed has an open character. On the other hand, where a space is strongly defined with a 'wall' above eye-level, the volume becomes more enclosed. However, the transparency or solidity of the structure affects the degree of enclosure, and this is an important consideration.

On warm summer days, spaces with only lightly sketched edges, perhaps achieved by lightly foliaged vegetation can be exhilarating. Strongly enclosed space, on the other hand, is 'a retreat to be sheltered and private in, to laze and recover in – or more mundanely, simply to escape from the wind. In such enclosed spaces, sensations such as the scent of plants, the texture of slight movement of leaves in the trees, are heightened.'[2]

Well-designed landscape enclosures can stress the contrast between the protected space enclosed and the outside world. If people within enclosures can enjoy near views or distant prospects, this adds to their appeal without detracting from the privacy of the spaces. Carefully framed views of distant objects help to provide a focal point from within a space, or punctuate a route passing through it. Spaces may be linked together to open out, from one to the next, giving a sense of anticipation, adventure and mystery.

The next chapter considers what can be achieved by enclosures and is followed by an analysis of the main types of hard-landscape materials used to form them. Enclosure with trees and hedges is considered in detail in Volume 1, *Soft Landscape*.

1. J. O. Simons, *Landscape Architecture – a manual of site planning and design*, (2nd edn.), McGraw-Hill, 1983.
2. Nan Fairbrother, *The Nature of Landscape Design*, Alfred A. Knopf, 1974.

CHAPTER 10

The Functions of Enclosures

Enclosures may be required to act as physical barriers, to provide visual screening, to reduce the effect of noise, impart privacy, shelter, safety, control of access and definition of ownership. Some enclosures may have to fulfil several of these functions simultaneously. For example, dry stone walls as field boundaries provide control of stock, shelter, definition of ownership and control of access. In fact, the walls, hedges and fences of field boundaries provide the greatest length of enclosing elements in the British Isles.

Landscape Enclosure and Subdivision

The subdivision of outdoor spaces and/or activities is an important aspect of landscape design. It is often desirable between potentially incompatible land uses, particularly in urban areas – for example, between sports pitches and, say, roads. Walls, fences, dense hedges, and planted or grassed banks are all effective means of achieving this end.

Noise Reduction

Screening to reduce noise levels requires a solid physical barrier to absorb or reflect the sound energy. This can be achieved by masonry walls, or carefully contoured mounds, sited close to the source of noise.

Foliage does not significantly reduce measured sound levels, but does reduce noise nuisance considerably. It helps to filter out atmospheric dirt, particularly along roads, and softens the visual impression of solid screens where they are not intrinsically attractive.

Privacy

Visual screening and privacy are synonymous when enclosure of private property is considered. In larger open spaces, such as parks or other public or semi-public areas, informal and locally private spaces can be created by the introduction of irregular edges to tree and shrub plantings. If correctly sited, these spaces form attractive sheltered niches that are the first spaces to be occupied when people come out to enjoy the sun. Conversely, large, flat civic spaces with poor enclosing elements often overlooked by many windows are obviously exposed and people feel uncomfortable within them. They are therefore likely to be underutilized.

Shelter

The landscape has been progressively modified and managed by man to make it more hospitable or useful. Simple enclosures have provided a shelter against the wind to benefit crop and livestock since the early days of organized agriculture. Shelter is a basic necessity of life and deserves a more central role in landscape design today. The value of shelter for buildings in exposed areas has been recently rediscovered. Savings in the annual heating costs of buildings at every scale, from domestic to industrial, can be made if the buildings are well sheltered. Shelter also makes life outdoors more comfortable in exposed areas and extends the number of days on which outdoor spaces can be used, for children's play or family relaxation, for example.

The provision of wind shelter has a wide range of other benefits, such as improving the safety of high-sided vehicles on exposed roads subject to strong winds. It can also protect footways, roads and railways from drifting snow, although the location and design of the wind shelter has to be worked out carefully if it is to be successful.

Copses and woodlands linked with the natural topography can provide excellent shelter (see Volume I, 'Soft Landscape'). In more exposed locations, forestry shelter belts protect settlements and crops. Triangular or three-legged shelter plantings offer farm animals protection on one side or another, whatever the wind direction. There are also many examples of efficient control of micro-climate at a smaller scale, such as walled gardens where tender plants can be grown on south-facing walls.

Solid barriers deflect wind and driving rain, but are most effective over a distance not greater than four times their height. They cause local turbulence, somewhat increasing windspeed further downwind and at each end of the barrier. Walls and boarded or slatted fences must be soundly constructed of durable materials to withstand the severe and abrupt wind pressures, including suction, that can be produced by gusts.

Permeable barriers can filter rather than deflect the wind and reduce wind strength on the leeward side without creating the turbulence that is caused by solid barriers. These can take several forms, such as perforated brick or concrete block walls and open-boarded fences, hedges and hurdles. However, these should be chosen carefully so that they are appropriate to the location.

Temporary shelter assists plant establishment and growth on exposed sites. In the past, wattle fences and hessian screens were used for this purpose, but now

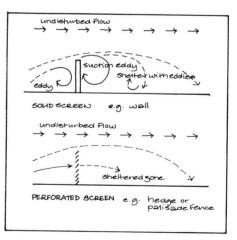

Figure 10.1   Diagram of wind patterns associated with free-standing solid and perforated screens.

Plate 1 The materials selected for this small, well-sheltered central London park has
helped to create a sense of repose.

Plate 2 In contrast to the previous illustration, the surface of this urban space is designed to allow for intensive pedestrian activity and low maintenance.

Plate 3 Gravel is an appropriate surface for formal places where traffic is light.

Plate 4   Cobbles make an attractive foil to garden plants.

Plate 5 South and west facing walls can be used to create a more hospitable microclimate for people and plants. Hedges perform a similar role but do not retain heat.

Plate 6 Contrasting hard landscape textures can be unified by having a common origin: in this case; natural stone.

polypropylene or polyethylene in perforated sheets or net form are a low-cost and easily removable alternative material. In time, shelter planting itself provides a more permanent form of protection for less hardy species.

Shelter in the landscape can also include covered walkways, bus and other small, roofed shelters. Where possible, park shelters should be sited to combine maximum wind shelter with good solar gain and good views, in order to encourage their use. The potential of shelter planting for reducing energy requirements in buildings, increasing comfort indoors and out and its values in landscape planning is considered in the 'Background' Chapter in Volume 1, *Soft Landscape*.

Safety

Enclosure is frequently used to provide essential protection in the form of safety barriers. It is, for example, important to prevent access to dangerous cliffs or rivers, and to prevent young children straying from supervised play areas. Skilfully designed enclosures can prevent danger by redirecting people's movements. This can be achieved in a number of ways, by the use of masonry walls, timber fences and hedges or expanses of low planting. Often the most effective barriers are simple and unobtrusive but protective barriers which could become play features are dangerous and this possibility should be considered at the design stage.

Control of Access

An entirely separate aspect of enclosure concerns protection of defensible space. By defining boundaries and making access difficult, it can be made quite clear that the space beyond is private. Where vertical elements would physically restrict the overall space and interrupt views, water can be a most effective and attractive barrier.

Definition of Ownership

Walls, fences, hedges and ditches often mark long-established boundaries. These features may be enshrined in the deeds of properties, describing the legal ownership or rights of access. Certain maintenance responsibilities may be required in the deeds, such as the repair or replacement of fences, ditch-cleaning or care of boundary trees. Unfortunately, legal boundaries are not always related to physical features on the ground and this can lead to misunderstandings over responsibilities for maintenance.

Definition of ownership can be achieved by subtle changes in level, planting, walls or by fencing. A dwarf hedge, low fence or posts may suffice. If the need is really only for boundary definition, the simplest way to achieve this is by use of markers flush with the ground, such as a change in paving material or a line of brass studs in paving.

Play Spaces

The type of enclosure is one of the key factors in determining the quality of a space's potential for play. Sympathetic design of the enclosing elements can create an appropriate scale of space, so that young children feel comfortable and secure. To be attractive to children, the play space should also be well sheltered. Moreover, young children are more sensitive to cold winds, intense sunshine and extremes of temperature than most adults. Shelter also encourages adults and the elderly to give informal play supervision, by providing for their reasonable comfort. The enclosing shelter should be arranged to maximize solar gain in winter and provide for some shaded play in summer. Entrances to play spaces should be preferably orientated to the south or south-west to prevent cold winds being funnelled in from the north and east.

Vegetation that is used to enclose play areas because it offers summer shade, winter shelter or visual variety should be protected from damage by children at play, at least until well established.

Safety must be a priority for play spaces and enclosing barriers are necessary to prevent children running out, on to adjacent roads. Robust barriers are also essential if there is any possibility of vehicles encroaching onto the playground.

It is desirable to provide enclosures with self-closing gates to exclude dogs, which tend to foul sandpits or lawns, particularly where young children play.

Figure 10.2   Enclosures can create outdoor rooms providing privacy and shelter.

Figure 10.3 Structures that can help enclose and screen pedestrian movement are valuable in residential areas.

CHAPTER 11

Walls

Walls are an important means of enclosure, particularly in town and village settings. Although comparatively expensive they do have the advantage of long life and low maintenance. Walls are particularly appropriate for relating outdoor spaces to buildings when both are constructed of the same materials.

Walls have certain key features in common, regardless of materials. All require sound foundations, and to be of sufficient thickness to ensure stability and to have a coping or capping to prevent the downward movement of water to the wall's interior.

Freestanding walls are liable to be overturned by wind forces, so their design should accord with sound principles of construction, such as those to be found in the Brick Development Association's publication entitled *Design of Free Standing Walls*. The advice of an engineer or suitably qualified person should be sought for freestanding walls over 1.8m high, for reinforced walls and for retaining walls over about 600mm high, and where the ground conditions may pose difficulties.

In designing a wall, it is necessary to consider:

1. the choice of materials to suit the function of the wall and the availability of materials appropriate to the locality;
2. wall stability – that is, resistance to high winds or vehicle impacts;
3. mortar specification, related to choice of building material, appearance, exposure and design details;
4. movement joints in walls more than about 7m long, to allow the wall to expand and contract without cracking;
5. copings or cappings to control the vertical penetration of water and to shed water;
6. damp-proof courses to control rising moisture.

These aspects are considered separately in the sections that follow.

Choice of Materials

Bricks

Bricks are made from clay, calcium silicate materials or concrete.

Clay bricks These provide the widest choice of colours, textures and densities. The colours range from off-white through greys, yellows, browns and reds to blue/black, depending on the clay material and the effects of firing. Textures vary from rustic hand-made bricks, through less coarse textures to smooth, extruded, wire-cut or machine-pressed bricks.

Clay bricks are not all of equal frost resistance. BS 3921:1985 'Specification for Clay Bricks' now under revision, defines the quality and categorizes three levels of frost resistance – two for external walls ('F' and 'M' categories) and one ('O' category) which is suitable for internal work only. It is worth noting that popular descriptive terms such as 'commons', 'facings', 'flettons' and 'engineering' bricks do not relate to frost-resistant characteristics in any dependable sense.

Either of the two frost-resistant categories, 'F' and 'M', may be used for freestanding and retaining walls. Bricks for exposed walls should be solid without the holes, slots or squares sometimes introduced to raise strength and speed up the firing. 'F' category bricks are frost-resistant where saturation and freezing might be expected. 'M' category bricks are moderately frost-resistant and are appropriate for use where the site is well sheltered and the detail design includes an effective overhanging coping.

Shortly after laying, some clay bricks may develop a white discolouration known as efflorescence. This is caused by salts present within the bricks being carried to the surface in solution and then drying on the face of the brickwork as a crystalline deposit with a white powdery appearance. This is generally caused by the bricks becoming saturated. Proper protection in storage and during construction reduces the risk of this occurring. The white salts generally weather away in subsequent rainfall.

Bricks may also be stained by lime from the ordinary Portland cement in the mortar, if not adequately protected during construction, or from concrete components above or behind them. This staining is difficult to remove as it requires careful acid treatment.

Calcium silicate bricks (BS 187) These are made from a mixture of lime and a sand or flint aggregate. Only approximately 5 per cent of bricks made in the UK are of calcium silicate, but they are cheaper and more uniform in size than clay bricks, although subject to considerable thermal shrinkage. Calcium silicate

Figure 11.1   Brick courses are incorporated into traditional knapped flint walls, providing rigidity and, incidentally, a pleasing contrast of colour and texture.

Figure 11.2 A squeeze stile in a dry-stone wall allows the passage of pedestrians but not livestock.

bricks of Class 3 strength and above possess good frost resistance, but higher-strength classes are recommended for cappings. Frost damage is severe in exposed situations, with the surface gradually eroding away. Their low-key character is valuable in garden walls where planting forms the main focus. For example, the soft buffs make an excellent background for subtle roses, where a richly coloured clay brick wall would compete. The silver-greys make a good foil for overhanging glossy evergreen leaves and rich red flowers or berries, like pyracantha or cotoneaster, and the near blacks throw white flowers into relief.

Concrete bricks These vary widely in quality but can be useful where a dense uniform product is required. They tend to shrink on drying: this factor should be reflected in the detail design.

Stone

Building stones are usually divided into three main groups, according to their origin or method of formation. Many factors influence the uses to which a building stone can be put. The two principal factors are, first, texture – that is, the general composition of the material which governs its workability and largely its weathering qualities – and, second, appearance.

Igneous rocks These were formed by volcanic activity below the surface of the earth. Granite, of which the chief constituents are quartz, mica and felspar, is the principal building material in this group.

Granite is a hard, weather-resisting material and is chiefly used where great strength is required or in places likely to receive heavy wear. Plinths or base courses of walls were often of granite, as were kerbs, protecting bollards and

Figure 11.3   In-situ concrete walls can be given a more interesting texture by the use of profiled formwork.

setts. They can be obtained in a variety of colours, including pinks, greens and greys, according to source. The quartz and mica which reflect light, give a degree of highlighting. Granites are comparatively expensive because of the cost of quarrying, shaping the stone and transport.

Sedimentary rocks Formed by deposits made under water, these include many materials like sands and clays. The principal stones in this group are limestones and sandstones. Limestone is composed chiefly of carbonate of lime. Sandstone, of which the chief ingredient is silica, owes its origin to the disintegration of older rocks.

Generally speaking, limestones are lighter in colour than sandstones and are usually near white, or in shades of cream or creamy brown, although some of the varieties formed from shells are much darker.

Most sandstones are good general-purpose building materials. The colours are usually muted but include warm reds, browns and buffs. The texture varies from very fine to very coarse according to the size of the grains of silica. The very coarse varieties are suitable for heavy engineering works, whilst the finer, more 'regular' stone can be used for all purposes, being particularly suitable for copings. The laminated varieties are extensively used for paving.

Limestone and sandstone are graded according to their durability. Some are suitable for the external walls of buildings where they are protected from excessive moisture, but may spall and fail as a result of frost damage in freestanding or retaining walls.

Metamorphic rocks These are rocks that have been changed in formation by heat and pressure. Originally they may have been either igneous or sedimentary rocks. Slate is the chief metamorphic rock used in landscape construction. As a walling or fencing material, slate is generally confined to its areas of origin.

Stone can be finished in a number of distinct ways: 'pitched' (roughly shaped with hammer and chisel); 'sawn', resulting in smooth faces and regular shapes; and 'textured', where the sawn surface is further worked, for example, to a ribbed pattern. Dry stone walls can be constructed in unworked stone, as found. They may be random or brought to courses, the latter creating a more formal effect.

Rough walling can be finished with rendering which gives good weather protection. Mixes should not be too strong; between 1:1:6 and 1:2:9 are suitable. Usually applied in two coats, the finish can be left smooth or treated in a number of ways to create an attractive texture. It is usually painted to provide additional weather protection and to improve its appearance. Keeping water out of rendered walls is particularly important as renderings are easily lifted by frost action – see page 100 'Copings and cappings'.

Concrete

Walling products include concrete blocks with self-coloured, plain or textured faces, openwork blocks, reconstituted imitation stone and large precast concrete walling units. External walling products to BS 6073, Part 1, are made with carefully controlled mixes and are frost-resistant. Plain concrete blocks are cheaper but on the other hand, precast textured or exposed aggregate blocks are more expensive than bricks. Stone is more expensive than either. Blocks are quicker to lay than bricks or stone, particularly irregular-sized blocks.

Plain blocks form a good plain background to plants which have an interesting texture. Blockwork walls can, if necessary, be rendered or painted to achieve a particular effect in order to marry in with adjacent buildings, existing walls or for additional weather protection.

Openwork blocks can be built up to form pierced screens that combine a degree of privacy with air circulation (valued in hot and humid climates) and support for climbing plants. Back lighting on a pierced screen wall can project interesting patterns on adjacent paving.

Imitation stone products can never equal the qualities of natural stone. Their principal disadvantage lies in the lack of subtle variations in texture and colour when compared with natural stone, except perhaps when viewed from a considerable distance. The reason for this is that the units are generally copies of a limited number of natural stones. Repeated endlessly, they fail to achieve the random surface texture that is one of the most attractive characteristics of natural stone. However, where the costs of using natural stone cannot be contained within a budget, the thoughtful use of this medium may be preferable to the use of other, less sympathetic, materials.

Concrete walls may also be cast *in situ*. In this country, however, the majority of plain *in situ* walls tend to become dirty, weather unevenly and stain badly, frequently resulting in a drab and depressing appearance. The surface may be given greater texture by, for example, casting the concrete against proprietary patterned or profiled formwork. The introduction of light and shade to the surface will help to create relief and interest. Alternatively, finer textures can be created if the aggregate is exposed by washing and brushing. The main disadvantages of this finish can be the difficulty of achieving uniformity of colour and texture, a problem that may be eased by the application of surface

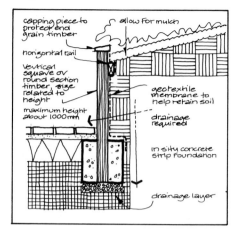

Figure 11.4   Section through low timber retaining wall. Dimensions will be determined by length, height and volume of retained soil.

retarders which do not cause significant damage to the coarse aggregate. The hardened concrete may also be tooled, which breaks away the outer surface to leave a rough-textured, durable finish. However, it is difficult to achieve uniformity of appearance and the process of exposing aggregate by this method is now largely superseded by surface blasting techniques. These processes reveal the colour of the coarse aggregate and so fundamentally change the appearance.

Timber

Low retaining walls (up to approximately 1m high) can be formed with durable timbers or softwoods which have been pressure-impregnated with preservative. Heavy section timbers, such as railway sleepers which have been pressure-creosoted, or peeled logs, are ideal for this purpose. For stability, the timbers can be driven directly into the ground at an angle or be set vertically, into a concrete foundation, to at least one-third of their length. The alignment of the timbers can be improved, and the structure stiffened, by being bolted to a horizontal timber rail on the rear face. The tops of the vertical timbers should be capped or weathered to shed water and so delay decay.

Timber retaining walls can also be built from factory-machined, interlocking units which have been treated with preservative.

Wall Stability

There are a number of ways of stiffening freestanding walls. The overall thickness of the wall itself can be increased, piers can be added or the form of the wall on plan can be given greater depth by creating staggered bays or by the introduction of simple curves. The pattern of piers can give visual relief to long walls and movement joints can be incorporated into them. It may also be important to consider the type of bond in relation to strength of construction.

A one-brick thick curved wall can be built in stretcher-bond with a minimum radius of 5m. Where space is limited, snapped header bond can reduce the radius to as little as 3m. Purpose-made splayed bricks may be used for tighter circles.

As a general guide, for freestanding walls not structurally linked to a building, less than 2.5m high and on normal soils, the foundation base level should be at least 600mm below finished ground level. On shrinkable clay soils a deeper foundation is usually necessary to avoid the effects of seasonal subsoil movement. Foundation thickness is commonly 225mm, and the foundation must be wide enough to achieve resistance to overturning due to wind and other superimposed loads. A brick wall 225mm wide typically requires a mass concrete foundation at least 525mm wide.

For freestanding brick walls on sloping ground, stepped foundations are required. The steps should be equivalent in height to the brick or block coursing. The length of the overlap in the foundation should be twice the depth of the step.

If possible, walls should not be located within the canopy of existing trees that are to be retained, in order to avoid damaging the root system. Where such an alignment cannot be avoided, the main roots should be retained intact by bridging the wall over them.

Retaining walls must be of sufficient weight, or be suitably reinforced, to resist being pushed over by the retained soil and the foundations must be designed to suit local ground conditions. Again, a suitably qualified engineer should design the wall.

In order to prevent water pressure building up behind the wall, a free-draining material should be used as backfill. A land drain should be laid in the bottom of the backfill and, in the case of short retaining walls, weepholes provided at regular intervals. The weepholes should be close to the base of the wall, as the water running from them may stain the surface. The top of the porous backfill should be covered with a layer of geotextile fabric to prevent fine sand and silt in the soil from gradually clogging the voids.

The rear face of a retaining wall should be thoroughly waterproofed to prevent water seeping through to the face. If not treated, this could cause spalling to moderately frost-resistant bricks, efflorescence or lime-staining from the mortar.

Figure 11.5   Low timber retaining walls provide an attractive planting terrace.

Figure 11.6 *Above:* Piers are used to stiffen free-standing brick walls.

Figure 11.7 *Below:* A practical method of carrying construction over major tree roots.

Retaining structures may also be constructed in interlocking unit components which can be stacked together with soil to retain and stabilize steep slopes. One method is to employ a crib structure, and proprietary products are available in timber and concrete. A disadvantage of this method can be the difficulty of retaining soil within the surfaces of the structure which is therefore exposed. Another technique is to use precast concrete units which retain their own parcel of soil. These are stacked and raked to provide spaces for the introduction of plant material. The advantages of both techniques is that they are relatively cheap when compared to solid structures and they can be attractive when covered with plants.

Mortars

Mortar mixes should be selected to suit the wall materials, exposure and design details (see BS 5628, Part 3, Section 22).

Table 11.1 Mortar Mixes

Mortar Designation	Type of mortar	Air-entrained mixes	
	Cement:lime:sand	Masonry cement: sand	Cement:sand with plasticizer
	Proportions by volume	Proportions by volume	Proportions by volume
(i)	1:0 to 1/4:3		
(ii)	1:½:4 to 4½	1:2½ to 3½	1:3 to 4
(iii)	1:1:5 to 6	1:4 to 5	1:5 to 6

Increasing resistance to frost attack during construction ....>

Improvement in adhesion and consequent

<.. resistance to rain penetration

Source: Table based on Table 15 Mortar Mixes in BS 5628:Pt.3.

Plasticizers are used to give greater workability to the mortar and can give some resistance to frost attack during the initial curing time, but they should not be relied upon to give protection against freezing. They can be detrimental to adhesion so the advice of a suitably qualified person should be sought before their use is considered.

For the selection of appropriate mortar mixes in relation to the construction and material used, refer to Table 13 of BS 5628 Part 3: 1985 'Code of Practice for the Use of Masonry'. If there is any doubt about the suitability of a mortar, advice may be sought from the stone quarry, brick or block manufacturer.

A sulphate-resisting Portland cement should be used below ground if sulphates are present in the groundwater. This requires a laboratory test for confirmation, although general advice may be available from the local authority. When 'FN' or 'MN' durability-designated bricks are used and are likely to be subjected to repeated saturation, a laboratory test must be carried out.

The mortar joints can be finished in a number of ways, the most common of which are recessed, flush, weather-struck or bucket-handle. The style of pointing affects the overall appearance of a wall considerably. Recessed pointing cannot be recommended since water lodging in the recesses can freeze and can cause arrises to spall off if an 'M' designated brick is used. Flush joints emphasize the form of the wall as a whole and require highly skilled workmanship. Weather-struck joints, characterized by a slight shadow produced by the recess at the top of the joint, are formed by compressing the mortar by drawing the tip of a trowel along the joint. The joint is thus formed to throw water down and out of the joint. Bucket-handle joints are a good compromise, draining water downwards, showing the texture of the surface and compressing the pointing to a smooth finish.

Coloured mortar can be used either to emphasize the joints or merge them with the wall material. Pointing mortars can be 'permanently' coloured by the use of coloured sand or, alternatively, may be tinted by the addition of pigments, although these may be prone to fade. However, it should be noted that the cement content must not be reduced under any circumstances.

Movement Joints

All building materials expand or contract due to the effects of variation in temperature and moisture. Clay products are particularly subject to thermal expansion. Unless controlled by movement joints, expansion can lead to cracking and structural failure. The general view is that vertical joints should be provided in freestanding walls at about 10m intervals for clay bricks and 6m or less intervals for calcium silicate and concrete bricks (see BS 5628, Part 3). These should be at least 10mm wide and go right through the wall including the coping. Joints should be carefully located so as neither to reduce the structural strength of walls nor to detract from their appearance.

Expansion joints in freestanding walls may be left open or filled with polyethlene foam compressed by 25 per cent on insertion into the joint. They may be pointed with a suitable non-setting mastic or polysulphide sealant. Oil-based mastics or sealants should not be used as they tend to harden and fall out. Coloured sealants are now available to match the mortar or wall material.

In concrete walls, shrinkage movement can be accommodated by the provision of 'control joints'. These are recessed, internal joints, where panels abut each other, closed by a polysulphide or mastic sealant.

Copings and Cappings

The basic function of a coping is to shed rainwater and to prevent downward water penetration into the interior of the wall and consequent risk of frost damage. Copings overhang and create a shadow line, which gives visual emphasis. If the overhang is at least 50mm and provided with a drip, the coping helps to prevent the top courses of the wall below from being saturated by driving rain. However, the designer should consider the visual effect of the coping as well as its waterproofing function.

A capping is of the same width as the wall below and does not provide the protection that a coping does.

Coping and capping bricks are available in frost-resisting, 'F' quality, to BS 3921. Typical cross-section shapes are: half-round, bullnose (single or double-sided), cant (single-and double-sided) and saddleback (triangular) sections.

At the ends of walls, the copings are exposed to weathering on three faces and are also vulnerable to removal through vandalism. Although they can be retained by non-ferrous metal cramps bonded into the wall, the cramps themselves are unattractive. A neater solution can be achieved by the use of a special square 'stop end' coping brick (square, bullnose or triangular), which has greater bonding area and weight, thus achieving a stronger joint. The use of an epoxy resin or styrene butadene rubber additive in the mortar improves adhesion. Many manufacturers make copings and cappings with an interlock between top and base sections, giving strong mechanical continuity.

Clayware ridge tiles are an attractive, effective and traditional coping material. As may be seen in some 1930's suburbs, colour-glazed tiles in blues, greens and yellows can make a vivid impact in the urban landscape, although they are now rarely used.

Concrete copings are excellent for concrete block or rendered walls, where a unified appearance is desirable. Plain concrete stains with age, unless the rainfall is very low, but this is less apparent with an exposed aggregate finish. Used on stone or brick walls, the precision of precast concrete clashes with their subtle surface modelling. Moreover lime from the concrete can permanently stain the brickwork below.

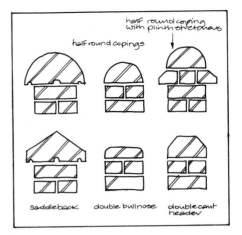

Figure 11.8 Preferred copings and cappings for free-standing brick walls.

A dressed stone wall may be finished with a suitable coping of dressed or sawn stone. In rural settings, stone walls are more traditionally finished with vertical or raked soldier courses.

In order to resist wilful damage, copings near ground level should be keyed in to the tops of walls or be of a preformed interlocking pattern so that they cannot easily be levered off.

Damp-Proof Courses

A damp-proof course is required at 150mm above ground level to prevent upward movement of moisture into the body of all walls not built of impervious material. Since the resistance of a freestanding wall to overturning is reduced by flexible damp-proof courses, because they do not bond well with mortar, the Brick Development Association recommends either two courses of clay engineering bricks or 'DPC Bricks', 'FL' quality or two courses of slates laid with a 1:3, cement:sand mortar mix. Both materials allow good adhesion across the joint. Granite or slate are the only stones which are sufficiently impervious not to require a damp-proof course.

A flexible damp-proof course is necessary below the majority of copings and cappings. If a flexible damp proof course is used in this situation it must have a rough-textured surface to give a good bond, otherwise it will weaken the joint and increase its vulnerability to vandalism. Damp-proof courses may also look untidy, so attempts are often made to conceal them with mortar – this defeats the object of the exercise as it allows moisture to bypass. A slate or tile 'creasing' course, which overhangs below a brick on edge or ridge tile coping, is used to shed water away from the surface of the brickwork below. Like a coping, it forms a shadow line which can be an attractive feature, but this form of construction may be used to incorporate a flexible damp-proof course to give adequate protection against the downward percolation of water into the wall below. An alternative approach is to build the entire wall in FL quality bricks to achieve a unified appearance.

A wall is only as good as its weakest component. Therefore, to ensure that the design for a landscape wall will work in practice, it is always best to have a sample length, completed in all details, built well in advance to determine what is acceptable from a construction, weathering and visual viewpoint. Skilled site supervision is also a particularly important aspect of all landscape construction that has to resist natural forces.

CHAPTER 12

Timber Fences

One of the pleasures of using timber in fencing is that it is a most versatile material which can be worked to suit a wide range of requirements. Vertical, diagonal or horizontal boards of equal or unequal spacing and varied widths, enable the achievement of designs which range from the subdued right through to the striking. Timber is an ideal material for coordinating buildings, enclosures and gates. Well detailed fences constructed of durable timber, and properly maintained, offer good life expectancy in relation to their cost.

Fences can be used to indicate property ownership and discourage casual trespass, but are not really suitable as a secure physical boundary. A close-boarded fence above eye-level can significantly improve shelter, and fences which are open in structure offer a measure of protection without obstructing the view. Certain forms of fencing, such as post and rail, or strained cleft chestnut, are well suited for reinforcing a young hedge which, when mature and properly managed, can take over to create a robust, long-term boundary.

Many traditional, well-proven styles of timber fencing are still used, but prefabrication and ease of erection now tend to influence design. An advantage of simple timber fences is that they can readily be repaired if sections are damaged or decay.

Materials

Timber for external use must either be naturally resistant to decay or, alternatively, be sufficiently permeable to allow adequate preservation treatment. The Timber Research and Development Association (TRADA) assesses durability in terms of five classes, based upon the average life of a 50 x 50mm cross-section of heartwood in contact with the ground as shown in Table 12.1.

Table 12.1   Life Span of Timber

Durability Class	Life Span	Examples
Very durable	more than 25 years	Greenheart
Durable	15–25 years	American mahogany
Moderately durable	10–15 years	European larch
Non-durable	5–10 years	European elm
Perishable	less than 5 years	most softwoods

When reliance is to be placed upon the natural durability of the timber, sapwood must be excluded, but where a preservative is applied, sapwood is permitted. Timber should be selected to avoid split, green or very knotted wood.

Softwoods are commonly used for fence construction because of their relatively low cost. All should be pressure-impregnated with preservative. Exceptions are larch heartwood, which is both moderately durable and strong, so is ideal for posts and rails, and western red cedar which is rather less hard and expensive, but is a pleasing colour and suitable for small board fences or trellises. Hardwoods are generally more expensive, but are used in some types of traditional fencing, such as riven oak rail fencing. Oak posts are specified for a wide range of timber fences because of their durability.

Timber preservative preparations fall into three groups: tar oils – for example, creosote applied by pressure-impregnation or by steeping in open tanks; pentachlorophenol in organic solvent by double vacuum; and water-borne copper/chrome/arsenic solutions by vacuum pressure. Creosote is one of the most effective and long-lasting preservatives, especially where the timber is below ground. It is, however, harmful to plants and it should not be used where roots or foliage would come into contact with it.

Fixings and fittings for timber fence construction and gates should generally be galvanized. Note that western red cedar and oak both stain in contact with iron and should therefore be used in association with non-ferrous fixings.

Careful design and detailing, such as weathering post tops and adding cappings and gravel boards to boarded fences can considerably enhance the life span of timber fences.

Timber Sizes

Hardwoods are generally available in thicknesses up to 150mm, widths of 150mm and over and lengths normally from 1.8m upwards.

Most European softwoods are available in thicknesses up to 100mm and widths of 75mm to 225mm. Lengths are normally available in 300mm increments up to about 5.7m, but greater lengths are sometimes available.

Finishes

All untreated timber eventually weathers to a silvery grey colour which may be acceptable where the timber is durable.

An expanding range of decorative, protective exterior finishes is available for timbers – namely paints, varnishes and exterior wood stains. Only the latter two enhance and preserve the natural appearance of wood. Exterior wood stains and permeable paints have been most extensively applied to softwoods but are also an appropriate finish for hardwoods.

Paints Paints are either gloss or matt finish and have the major advantage of hiding surface blemishes, such as repairs. Conventional, oil-based film-forming paints should only be used where adequate preparation and, most importantly, frequent and thorough maintenance is assured. Products that are moisture-permeable and non-film-forming are to be preferred since they give a longer life.

Varnishes The Timber Research and Development Association (TRADA) does not recommend the use of hard varnishes for use on exterior woodwork because of the rapid film breakdown and resultant staining.

Exterior wood stains These are generally transparent, so that the wood grain remains visible. Wood stains are either water or organic solvent-based and are available in a wide range of bright colours, as well as 'natural' wood colours. They perform better on sawn, as opposed to smooth-planed, timber. Although wood stains contain some preservative, an initial penetrating treatment with a compatible wood preservative is recommended.

The major advantage of wood stains is that maintenance is relatively straightforward. They gradually fade, rather than flake, so maintenance depends largely upon what is an acceptable level of colour change.

Timber Fencing Types

Cleft chestnut paling (BS 1722, Part 4, 1972)

This type of fencing is prefabricated and comprises hand-split sweet chestunut uprights or 'pales' between 900mm and 1800mm high, evenly spaced and wired together top and bottom. It is normally supported by softwood or chestnut posts at intervals of up to about 2.5m for temporary use, but it can be attached to a timber post and rail fence for greater strength.

Its main advantages are versatility, relative cheapness, ease of erection and potential for re-use. It can look at home in both town and country and be used on variable slopes. It is widely used for temporary protection of areas of construction or soft landscape works.

Timber post and rail fencing (BS 1722, Part 7, 1972)

This can be used successfully in many locations yet, where it is high with several rails, it can appear too dominant, for instance on rural roadsides where a

Figure 12.1   Split oak post and rail fencing is a tradition of south-eastern England. Note that the rails are morticed into the posts.

more lightweight timber post and wire fence would be less assertive. However, with careful selection of the appropriate detail design, size of timber and finishes, this type of fencing can be a visual asset in many situations, the three-rail fences being the most restful to the eye.

Post and rail fencing is usually constructed by nailing the rails to the posts, which may be rebated to accept the rails. However, in the best work, they are morticed into the posts and secured by hardwood dowels. In nailed construction, the centres of the posts should be at intervals not exceeding 1.8m and the widest face of the post should be in contact with the rails. The nails should be galvanized and ringed to resist pulling out. Joints in rails should occur at alternate posts. However, when the rails are morticed into the posts, the widest face of the post should contain the mortice and the post intervals can be increased up to 2.70m, centre to centre.

A particular type of post and rail fence is the low guard, or trip rail fence, used typically to protect planting areas. They are also effective in channelling pedestrian movement in large open spaces such as parks to prevent erosion next to a footpath. They are generally 300–400mm high and can be constructed with heavy oak posts in concrete where damage from cars may be anticipated. Typical post sizes are 200mm x 150mm, 150mm x 150mm, and 100mm x 100mm, at between 1,000mm and 1,500mm centres. The rails should be weathered to shed water and to discourage children from walking along them. Rail sizes vary from 150mm x 50mm, 150mm x 100mm to 100mm x 100mm. The rails may be fixed to the posts by metal straps or bolted.

Ranch-style fences

These are similar to post and rail, except that the rails and spaces are of equal widths. Having enjoyed a passing vogue in residential areas, this type of fence has become a cliché, and is now less frequently used. The commonest design is based on two wide rails. Careful selection of timber sizes and colouring together with setting-out which avoids long wavering runs, can result in a reasonable appearance.

Closeboarded and palisade fences

These are post and rail fences with the addition of boarding or pales. BS 1722, Parts 5 and 6, 1972 apply to closeboarded and palisade fences. A high,

Figure 12.2 Boards on the diagonal are an attractive alternative to the traditional, vertical close-boarded fence styles.

Figure 12.3 A close-boarded fence design that cleverly avoids having front and back faces.

closeboarded fence is a relatively low-cost means of defining a boundary and it is one of the few fences to provide visual screening. Planting can be combined with the fence to soften its appearance. Closeboarded fences are constructed from vertical lengths of overlapping feather-edge boards. Alternatively, rectangular boards can be applied to both sides of the horizontal rails to form a 'hit and miss' fence which will block views straight through but allows some air movement to take place.

The palisade or 'military' fence palings are pointed or flat-topped, and rectangular or triangular in cross-section. They are evenly spaced with gaps of about 50mm.

Variations on the traditional styles, including boards on the diagonal, are appearing more frequently as an attractive alternative. Traditionally, low palisade fences have been used for garden boundaries and often painted white. This should only be considered today where regular long-term maintenance is assured since, once painted, they are difficult to treat in any other way.

Closeboarded and palisade fences are reasonably rigid and stable. Three arris rails are necessary where the fencing is over 1,200mm high, and the boards or pales must be strong enough not to break if pulled from behind. Wherever domestic security is the main purpose of the fence, the palings should be set no more than 45mm apart, to prevent toe-holds being gained on the horizontal rail behind.

The tops of posts and the horizontal rails should be chamfered to shed water. The tops of vertical boards can be capped to avoid rot in the end grain. Gravel boards are a traditional feature at the bottom of closeboarded fences, where decay is likely due to the timber being in contact with the ground. They are attached to the posts and to a peg midway between, and can be replaced separately without disturbing the whole fence.

Prefabricated panel fences (BS 1722, Part 11, 1972)

These may be made of interwoven slats, vertical overlapping boarding or horizontal waney-edge boarding. The traditional fence panel is the hurdle, made of split hazel. These were originally manufactured for temporary stock fencing and are still available. Most timber fencing panels are manufactured for domestic use and they are not sufficiently durable for more demanding situations.

Vertical or horizontal louvred panels

These can be set in a frame to create an interesting and selective glimpse of the world beyond. The louvres should be set at an angle in a frame of sufficiently generous proportions to achieve the required degree of privacy, considering relative eye and ground levels.

Trellis

Either combined with other fencing, or set above it, trellis offers a pleasing and variable form of spatial division. It can be very open, and scarcely noticeable, or be made up of deep sections set close together so that it appears almost solid in oblique views. The potential for design variations is considerable. Lightweight, prefabricated forms are widely available, but are generally more appropriate for domestic use. More durable designs for specific needs should be purpose-made. Trellis is ideally suited for supporting a wide range of climbing plants and can be linked with pergolas and other overhead structures to help give light enclosure.

Figure 12.4   A painted timber fence which is lively and unusual.

Figure 12.5   A painted picket fence requires regular maintenance but can be appropriate in private gardens.

Figure 12.6   A pleasing and unusual timber fence with two front faces.

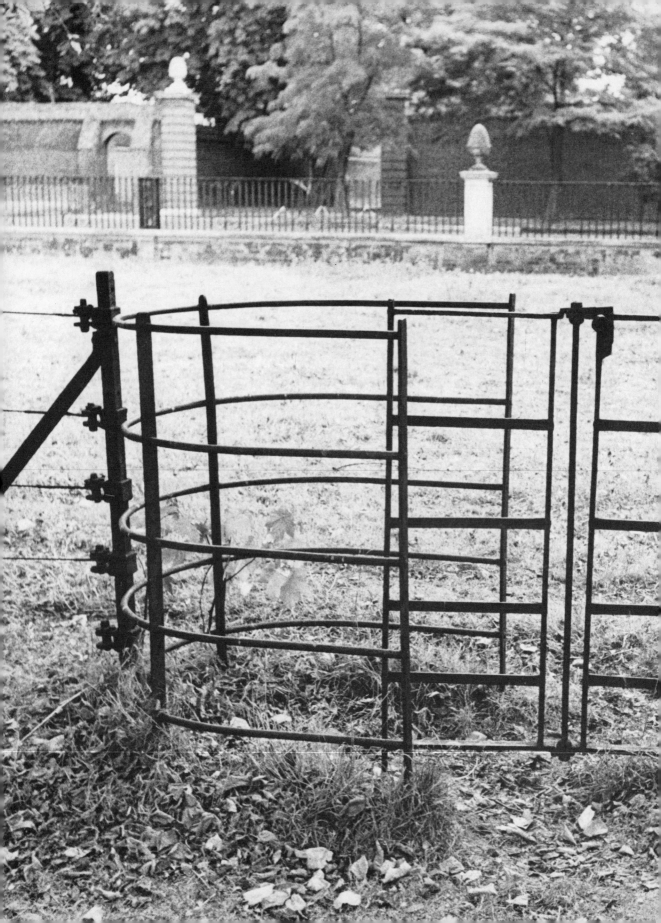

CHAPTER 13

Wire Fences

Strained Wire Fences

Strained wire fences (BS 1722, Part 3) are more widely used for defining boundaries in rural areas wherever there is less need for shelter or for privacy. They can provide temporary protection for areas of soft landscape during building or civil engineering contracts, and can also be used to reinforce a hedgeline during the 9–18 month establishment period, where trampling is expected. The height, number of horizontal wires, and post and 'dropper' spacings, depend on the function of the fence. Different patterns have evolved in agriculture to achieve an effective barrier for different types of stock.

Posts can be timber, concrete or metal. Timber is generally the most sympathetic material for use in the countryside and may be economically obtained locally. Tubular metal posts are neat due to their small size, made possible because of their strength. They are also appropriate in urban settings where their life is likely to be longer than that of timber. Conventional concrete posts, particularly when unweathered, look intrusive in almost any location.

Straining posts with struts are necessary at the ends of wire fences, at regular intervals and at every change of direction. Metal and concrete posts need to be set in a concrete foundation; timber posts can be driven directly into firm ground but, on loose or made-up ground, they should similarly be set into concrete. The fence wires are tensioned to remove any slackness by adjustable ratchets or eyebolts. Rolls of perforated polyethylene sheet can be attached by specialized proprietary fixings or simply tied to straining wires to form an effective horticultural windbreak, providing economic, temporary protection for young plants on more exposed sites during their establishment period. It is important to ensure that high tensile steel wire is used to achieve adequate straining to resist the affects of windage on such fences.

Woven Wire Fences

The woven wire fence (BS 1722, Part 2) has both horizontal and vertical wires, forming a square or rectangular mesh, and it can also be strained. It is used widely in agriculture as stock fencing. Various aperture sizes and overall heights are available for cattle, pigs, sheep or horses. Deer fencing has a much wider mesh and needs to be 1.8m high to discourage deer jumping over into woodland or plantations, for example.

It is a practical and economical rural fence and also makes a firm foundation for an informal hedge of, say, rambling roses, pyracantha or honeysuckle, which will grow through and eventually act as camouflage.

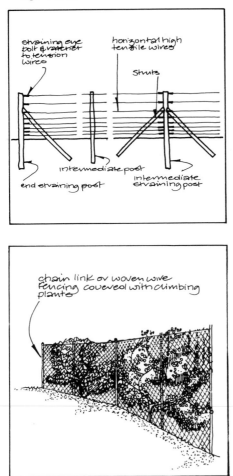

Figure 13.1   Strained wire fence.

Figure 13.2   Chain link fence can provide a firm foundation for climbing plants.

Chain Link Fences

Chain link is available for fences varying in height from 900mm to about 3.0m. The gauge of the mesh varies from medium to extra heavy duty, depending upon whether it is to used be for domestic or security purposes. The mesh can be galvanized or coated in PVC to extend its life. The PVC coating is available in a limited range of colours.

The posts may be timber, circular or square section steel tubes or concrete. The latter are widely used. The taller metal or concrete posts which form part of security fences are available with cranked tops. The steel angle or tee-shaped sections tend to rust too readily in the corner. The chain link mesh is supported by a minimum of three strained line wires at 0.9m high with additional wires, depending on the height of the fence.

In terms of appearance, the black plastic coated mesh on slender tubular black metal posts is the least obtrusive and merges most successfully with many backgrounds. The same is not true, however, for the heavy precast concrete posts which always look ugly in contrast with the green colours of the landscape.

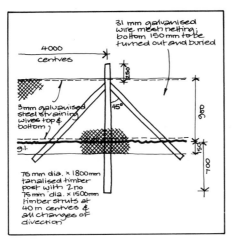

Figure 13.3   A rabbit-proof fence, with 150mm of mesh buried below ground.

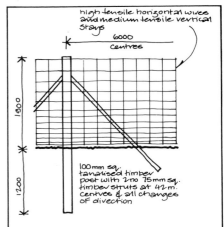

Figure 13.4   A deer-proof fence of woven wire.

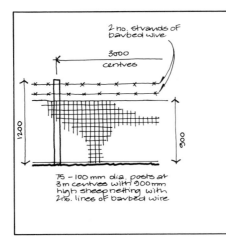

Figure 13.5   A stock fence suitable for sheep and cattle.

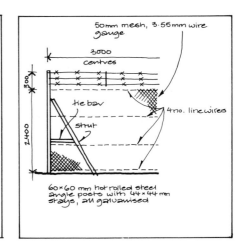

Figure 13.6   A high security fence.

Welded Mesh Fences

Welded mesh fences are factory-fabricated and made from mild steel wire welded together. Several different types of supporting posts are available. This type of fence is more effective for security fences than chainlink. Improved resistance to deformation is achieved by the prescence of a 'V'-shaped profile along the top and bottom of each panel. An increasing range of products appearing on the market which offer a variety of design opportunities.

CHAPTER 14

Metal Railings and Fences

Metal railings and gates have a long history, and new designs continue to be developed by designers and craftsmen, typically represented by the British Artist–Blacksmith Association. Traditional patterns in cast or wrought iron continue to be used in many older towns and cities and Victorian agricultural railings have remained in use in the countryside. The high resistance of metal railings to vandalism or accidental damage and decay, coupled with advances in technology and production, have encouraged a revival of interest in this type of fence.

The range of metal railings available today is wide, including traditional styles, prefabricated modern products and purpose-made designs. Each is appropriate to particular uses and locations. Complex, rich designs should be reserved for focal points, like gates, with a simple approach being applied to railings generally.

Materials

Cast Iron

Cast iron is an alloy of iron, carbon and silicon. It suffers less from rusting than wrought iron or mild steel and is more tolerant of chemical, salt or sand action. The major drawback of cast iron was its brittleness and low tensile strength, making cast iron railings more susceptible to fracture on impact. Cast iron is now manufactured in two qualities – namely, high-grade grey iron and ductile (SG). Ductile iron is superior to cast iron in tensile strength and will actually deform rather than break. The grey iron casting is suitable for bollards where there is a greater mass, whereas the ductile iron should be used for fence posts or other thinner section items.

Improvements in manufacturing techniques allow many impurities to be eliminated, leading to far greater tensile strength, so that modern cast iron is more likely to bend than to break.

It is now possible to weld cast iron in a workshop and, with care, even *in situ*, using special alloys. As the failure of old railings is often due to the corrosion of related fittings, such as mild steel screws, rather than in the cast iron itself, repairs should be considered before replacement. Screws should be stout and made of best-quality stainless steel. Electrolytic corrosion is often caused at the foot of railings where they have been secured in stone cills by molten lead. Care

Figure 14.1   Contemporary craftsmen blacksmiths can produce excellent 'one-off' designs such as this garden gate.

needs to be taken in selecting all types of metal fixings for metal objects since a combination of dissimilar metal accelerates corrosion.

Existing railings in reasonably good condition can be used as the pattern for replacements. The existing wide range of cast iron railings offers a source of design inspiration, but expert advice from a skilled pattern-maker is recommended at an early stage, since the construction of the moulds is the most expensive item in the manufacturing process.

Wrought Iron

Wrought iron is now uncommon, since what is commonly termed wrought iron is, in fact, wrought steel. As such it is resilient, highly malleable and can be worked easily into railings, gates, seats, trellises or even arbors. Cost can be high because the working of ornate designs is labour-intensive.

Mild Steel

Mild steel is a highly elastic and malleable material, products of which are manufactured in a variety of forms, including rolled sections, such as angles, and extruded sections, such as circular or square tubes, solid squares or rounds. These sections are used for production of posts, rails and frames for fencing panels.

Larger fence panels can be made in mild steel than was possible with traditional cast or wrought iron work. The hollow box sections or tubes give greater strength at lower cost. The dimensions of the galvanizing bath limit the maximum sizes that can be dipped. Mild steel is particularly prone to rust and needs to be galvanized to protect it from rusting. This treatment should be carried out as part of the manufacturing process. On-site work, such as cutting or welding, should be avoided as it breaks the integrity of the galvanizing surface film.

Aluminium

Aluminium is an attractive railing material, valued for its lightness, high strength and long life, despite its greater cost. It is approximately one-third the weight of steel and is far more resistant to structural corrosion than most other metal. A broad range of extrusions – for example, rods, flats, tubes and hollow box sections – is available, allowing designers to create a variety of factory-made railing panels. Because of the difficulty of manufacture, aluminium railings cannot easily be made on-site as a one-off design as can mild steel.

Designs, such as gates, can also be cast in aluminium. Untreated aluminium oxidizes to form a white patina on the metal that protects it from further deterioration. However, since it also collects dirt, the surface is usually painted or anodized to provide a good finish.

Metal Railing Patterns

Bar or Estate Fences (BS 1722, Part 8)

Mild steel or wrought iron continuous-bar fencing has long been used for enclosure on farms and in parklands. It is attractive and its simple robust character suits modern buildings, and perhaps deserves greater consideration for urban use.

Continuous-bar fencing and matching gates are manufactured in a range of heights and weights, for a variety of functions. A light, 1.05m high fence is suitable for enclosing sheep, whilst a 1.35m high, heavy-duty version is available for larger stock. An extra-strong model may be most appropriate for use in urban situations, where people may sit on the top bar.

The five or six horizontal bars can all be round-section, or the top bar only, with flat bars below. Joints in the horizontal bars must occur at posts. Square section posts measuring 50 x 50mm with 4mm thick walls, supported on a flat base plate below ground, stiffen the fence at intervals and at corners. The intermediate posts are either flat bars measuring 38 x 8mm, in which case they have a pronged foot underground to stabilize them, or T-section, with wing-plates welded onto the bottom. The mild steel can be protected with a galvanized, paint or plastic finish. This fence type can be easily adapted to

Figure 14.2   Recently installed steel railings designed to complement 19th century buildings.

Figure 14.3   Mild steel, hollow, box sections are a strong, inexpensive railing and fencing material which can be used in a variety of situations.

irregular topography, since horizontal curves and slopes can be accommodated, the limiting factor being the bending of the top bar.

Vertical Railings (BS 1722, Part 9)

Vertical bar fences are now generally manufactured from mild steel, rather than wrought iron, with square, round or triangular sections linked normally by only two horizontal rails top and bottom. Panel lengths vary from about 1.8m to 3.0m with heights from 0.6 to 2.4m. Although the higher panels are difficult to climb, posts should be strong enough to be able to withstand this and struts may be added if required. Both posts and struts are set into concrete foundations. If the verticals are to be carried above the top rail, the 'hairpin' looped type is safest, since accidents may occur if the verticals terminate above the horizontal rail in plain ends or spikes. Panels can be fabricated to follow uniformly sloping ground with vertical posts and raked top and bottom rails.

Palisade Fencing (BS 1722, Part 12)

Palisade fencing is constructed from cold-formed, corrugated mild steel pales fixed to angle section horizontal rails top and bottom. Posts are usually constructed of rolled or hollow steel sections set in concrete foundations at approximately 2.5m to 3.0m centres. As with all mild steel products, all the materials should be galvanized and may also be painted. This type of fencing acts as a more effective deterrent to the casual intruder than the vertical railing fence but is unlikely to be appropriate to high security requirements. It is available in heights between approximately 1.5m and 3.5m. The ends of the pales may be shaped to enhance their degree of deterrence.

Figure 14.4   Vertical railings can provide a high level of security.

Plate 7   The use of sturdy, traditional materials, such as timber and cast iron, seems particularly apt in a dockside location.

Plate 8 A strong, elegant metal railing, an appropriate design response to the opportunities of a water frontage.

Plates 9 & 10   Two examples of a sensitive blending of materials.

Plate 11 Landscape around buildings should be designed to reflect their architectural style, using complementary materials.

Plate 12 The use of in-situ concrete paving encourages the designer to express the flowing patterns created by people walking.

Figure 14.5 A 'trip-rail' can protect grass or planting from pedestrians taking a short cut, but a mowing strip detail is essential.

Figure 14.6 Traditional wrought iron vertical railings complement a park or garden setting in urban areas.

Horizontal Rails

Horizontal rail fencing has a number of applications, the most common of which is to control pedestrian movement. It can range from a relatively low barrier such as a trip rail, 300mm to 400mm high and adjacent to an area of planting, up to a taller, three-or four-rail barrier adjacent to, say, a sharp change of level. In both cases this type of barrier does not prevent access to the space as they can be stepped or climbed over or crawled under by small children. When a more positive barrier is required, then other types of fencing should be considered, such as vertical railings.

This type of fence is generally constructed with tubular steel posts and rails either clamped or welded together. Where more traditional materials are appropriate, a wide range of cast iron or cast aluminium posts with tubular metal rails are available. In some locations, chains may be more attractive than rails.

Prefabricated panels

These are usually constructed of rods, square or flat section mild steel, welded together in the factory to form panels. The panels are usually bolted to flat or square hollow-section mild steel posts set in concrete. Panels are manufactured in a wide range of sizes and design to suit a wide range of applications, from simple pedestrian protection to security fencing. As with other mild steel products, they should be galvanized and may be painted.

Figure 14.7 Pre-fabricated metal panels create a strong sense of enclosure.

PART III

Landscape Furniture

CHAPTER 15

Landscape Furniture

This section of the Guide deals with the selection and siting of outdoor 'furniture' and related landscape fittings. The aesthetic appeal of specific items varies widely from person to person and this Guide should not be thought of as a 'catalogue of good taste'. It is hoped to stimulate readers to select attractive, functional products and to consider sensitive ways of using them together in order to create interesting and imaginative urban landscapes.

There are many instances where uncoordinated landscape furniture and fittings bring visual confusion to the street scene, which could be resolved by a coherent design policy. Coordinated ranges of seats, benches, litter bins, signs and light fittings, help to unify a landscape scheme, but it should be remembered that 'ranges' can go out of production.

Visual clutter outside the designer's control can be created by statutory undertakers, like the water, gas and electricity boards and British Telecom, which each have standard equipment or markers which must be incorporated into many developments. Their siting is often governed by regulations, so it is important to obtain information about these early in the design process.

The careful location of landscape furniture is also critical, both to its functional efficiency and to the appearance of the scene as a whole. For example, it is not sensible to position seating in a draughty outdoor 'wind tunnel'.

Landscape furniture can be subjected to considerable wear and tear. Its suitability for a particular scheme can be assessed by studying examples that have been in use for several years in comparable situations.

Once landscape furniture has been installed, regular inspection is essential as the efficient and speedy repair of damage in public places is important to prevent injuries, is a means of generating respect for the environment and discourages thoughtless damage or outright vandalism. To ensure good value for money when selecting landscape furniture, continuing maintenance costs (replacement, servicing, painting and so on) need to be balanced against capital expenditure, along with achieving the desired visual and functional requirements.

In almost any setting where landscape furniture is used, it is desirable to move towards a design that achieves harmony between the individual elements of landscape furniture and the landscape of the setting. The trees, pavings and surrounding architecture all integrate with the selected products: the result should be of positive environmental benefit.

CHAPTER 16

Sitting Outdoors

Siting

The first impression of a sitting place is important. The careful grouping of seats in the right setting creates an appropriate ambience and sense of place.

First, is the outlook attractive? Advantage should be taken of the site character or particular features. For example, there may be unexpected views through the branching tracery of a weeping tree, views that catch the play of sunlight on rippling water or a vista framed by an archway.

Second, is it comfortable? Comfort should extend from good ergonomic design of the seats or benches themselves, to wind shelter and protection from noise and from the mud or water sprayed up from passing vehicles. To allow people to enjoy seats in winter, some should be placed in the shelter of a hedge or massed shrubs, in the recesses of indented walls or in simple roofed shelters. In Britain, these protected seats should preferably face between south-east and south-west, to take advantage of the brief periods of winter sunshine. In summer, carefully placed deciduous trees with light foliage can be used to give moderate shade to south-facing sitting places in a way that avoids blocking off welcome winter sunshine. An open tracery of branches lets sunlight through to dry off the dew of early summer mornings and summer showers. However, species that exude leaf drip, such as lime, or have fruits and berries attractive to birds, should obviously not overhang seats.

Third, is the sitting place accessible? Where seats are placed on raised ground to take advantage of a fine view, for example, access should be by sufficiently wide paths, at easy gradients, so that elderly or disabled people and those with prams can enjoy them.

To provide clearance for people walking in front, seats should be set back at least 0.5m from the edges of paths. Generally, seats should stand on firm, well-drained, hard paving so that it is dry and free from puddles. If the likely wear on grass is low, as in rural areas or private gardens, paving may be unnecessary. It is sometimes sensible to site litter bins nearby.

Artificial illumination of seating areas not only attracts people in the evenings but helps to ensure their safety and comfort (see Chapter 21).

Finally, does the seating arrangement encourage sociability? A conversation corner can be created by placing together a number of three to four-person fixed benches or seats. Semi-circular arrangements of seats also help to create a sociable setting. Circular or hexagonal seats can be used around mature trees.

Design

Seats need not always be formal, manufactured items. Broad steps, low walls, or gently sloping, south facing grass banks can provide informal sitting areas for large numbers of people to relax in summer sunshine. For instance, the grass slopes at North London's Kenwood House leading down to the lake provide seating for thousands at evening concerts every year. Similarly, the grassy banks of Cambridge's River Cam are well used for informal recreation on warm days without spoiling the view of the river for strollers during the rest of the year.

Conventional seats used in public areas should be securely fixed to the ground or to sheltering walls. Although single unfixed seats allow for the maximum flexibility of use, the likelihood of theft restricts their use to supervised areas.

Where people seek only brief periods of rest (for example, at a bus stop), seats can be simple benches or 'perches', but relaxed contemplation and sociability cannot be enjoyed without comfortable backrests.

Fear of possible wilful damage should not deter a positive approach to the use of seats in landscape design. Their potential for enhancing the richness of landscape experience should largely override fears of misuse.

While the design of conventional manufactured seats continues to evolve, the traditional patterns of hardwood and cast iron park benches are still found attractive and practical by many. These are well-tried designs, supported by a revival in the production of furniture. The simpler versions are helpful pointers to good modern seat design.

Seats should not only have a pleasing appearance and be comfortable, but they should also be durable, strong and simple in construction to reduce vandalism and minimize maintenance. Structural weaknesses such as inadequate welding, or over-generous spans of timber, should be avoided to prevent injury or breakages – malicious or otherwise. The timber should always be of selected quality and should be a non-splintering, straight grained species, planed and sanded with all edges in contact with users rounded or chamfered.

The best timbers for seats are naturally decay-resistant, such as oak, teak or oiled iroko. Alternatively, pressure-treated softwoods can be used. There is an ethical advantage in selecting home-grown hardwoods rather than imported ones. Irreparable damage done to tropical rain forests by loggers removing a handful of trees and devastating large areas in the process cannot now be justified in providing hardwood for seats and other uses in this country.

Timber can be left to weather naturally or it can be stained in a range of attractive colours. Painted sitting surfaces are practical but are expensive to

Figure 16.1   Seats need not be manufactured items. These benches look good because they are an integral part of the walls or paving around them.

Figure 16.2   This simply designed, robust, granite seat is perfectly integrated with its setting of granite setts and wall.

Figure 16.3   Seats should be both pleasing in appearance and comfortable.

maintain since they require regular repainting to avoid unsightly disfigurement caused by weathering.

Cast iron frames from classical moulds have regained popularity. Although they have high initial costs, they are more corrosion-resistant than mild steel products. Painted, galvanized steel frames are widely used with timber slats. Stainless steel frames can be attractive in an urban setting. Precast concrete frames with timber slats make robust seats, but are arguably less elegant than well-designed metal or timber seats because of their tendency to be heavy in appearance.

Newer materials, such as moulded plastic or perforated metal mesh, coated in PVC to provide greater protection against decay, are becoming widely used alternative materials for frames and seat surfaces. Fire damage is perhaps least with seats made entirely from concrete or pressed stainless steel.

In rural areas, low-cost materials reflecting the regional character can provide an attractive solution – for instance, slate slabs in Wales, granite in Scotland and halved tree trunks in lowland areas.

Details of construction which appear to be minor can be deceptively important. For example, screws, nuts and bolts should be corrosion-resistant, and they should be recessed and plugged to prevent injury and to discourage unauthorized dismantling. All mild steel, exposed or otherwise, should be fully protected by galvanizing or equivalent method, to avoid staining and corrosion.

Maintenance

Damage can be reduced when the public can see that the owners of seats, or the local authority responsible for them, repairs them promptly. Therefore, the products in use and their components should be kept readily available from local stores, or on call from the manufacturers' stock. Regular inspection is necessary to check on safety, decay or vandalism. Adjacent sheltering plants or overhanging trees may require pruning from time to time.

CHAPTER 17

Plant Containers

Today, planting in containers on paved surfaces has become a popular feature of pedestrian spaces in many city centres. Plants in containers should only be used where they can positively enhance a particular urban environment. All too often they are used merely as space fillers or barriers, instead of being an integral part of the overall design.

Permanent planters, containers or raised beds are comparatively expensive, and they can incur higher maintenance costs through additional irrigation and fertilizer requirements. They do not always provide ideal conditions for plant growth, so they should be used where ground-level planting is not feasible or would be liable to damage.

Design

Plant containers should be selected and grouped to reflect the character of the landscape setting in terms of size, shape, and materials. They can be designed also to serve as seats as well as effective barriers. There are a number of situations where containers are particularly useful.

1. Where ground-level planting is likely to be trampled.
2. Where vehicle traffic in a confined area might manoeuvre, or short-cut over planting at ground level – for example in car parks and entrances – or where fast-moving traffic would spray ground-level planting with road salt – for example, alongside urban arterial roads. Plant containers lower than 1.0m should be kept well away from road spray.
3. Where plants cannot be grown directly in the soil, e.g. on flat roofs, balconies, raised walkways and decks in civic or shopping centres.

Permanent planters must be located clear of existing underground service runs and any new services should be routed around them, since future excavations underneath planters would be impractical. Access for horticultural maintenance or for relocation of movable containers should be considered when siting planters.

In order to avoid drainage water discolouring the pavement, movable containers should be sited close to, or over, surface drainage points or channels. Alternatively they can be placed over a bed of gravel or dark engineering bricks.

Materials and Construction

Like other street furniture, plant containers benefit from a simple appearance and robust construction.

Figure 17.1   Balcony and roof planting provides a welcome outlook from city windows.

Raised planting beds constructed *in situ* of brick, stone, concrete or timber should be designed to relate to the proposed levels or contours, site character, local materials and the other landscape furniture within the same scheme. For maximum flexibility in design, containers in stacking sections are available so that the height and volume can be varied to suit a wide range of shrubs and trees.

Planters should be resistant to frost, root action, vandalism and rough treatment during relocation.

Mass-produced portable containers are available in a variety of materials. Glass-reinforced concrete is relatively light and has a smooth, easily cleaned finish. Precast concrete is cheaper, but has to be cast about four times thicker than glass-reinforced concrete to achieve the same rigidity and is thus heavier. Precast concrete has a rougher surface but this can be finished with an exposed aggregate (which can be useful for matching other elements in the scheme). Moulded glass-reinforced plastic is versatile in shape and colour. Being smooth, it is also easy to clean, although certainly less robust.

Also available is a wide range of well-made and attractive timber containers. Metal containers are liable to corrode and so usually require an inert liner, adding to the cost. Terracotta containers are only suitable for external use if they are frost-resistant and if there is no risk of impact damage. The supplier's advice should be sought on frost resistance.

Prefabricated plant containers must have adequate drainage holes. The base of the plant container should contain a drainage layer, at least 50mm thick, of clean, coarse gravel (without fines). The growing medium should be separated from the drainage layer by a filter mat, to prevent finer particles working down and gradually blocking the drainage layer. Where the loading on building structures must be minimized, lightweight, synthetic drainage materials can be substituted for gravel and special lightweight soil mixtures used.

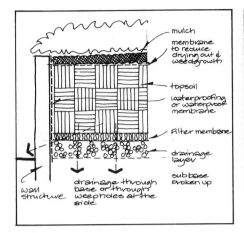

Figure 17.2 *Above:* Section through layers within a planter.

Figure 17.3 *Right:* This box of rugged timbers contrasts well with the crisp lines of the brick paving.

Permanent raised beds in contact with the natural ground are the most satisfactory for plant growth. The root systems can expand more freely which will reduce vulnerability to drought, increase the nutrient supply and improve anchorage.

Existing ground in the base of *in situ* planters should be properly cultivated, before backfilling with growing medium, to facilitate natural drainage and root penetration into the soil below. *In situ* planters require weepholes near the base of their walls for drainage if subsoil drainage cannot be provided.

Plant Selection

The key points to bear in mind in selecting plants, in addition to the available space and costs, are the prevailing micro-climate and the degree of maintenance that can be reasonably expected. In practice, plants in containers often have to cope with poor maintenance, compacted soil, nutrient deficiency and uncertain water supply.

CHAPTER 18

Signs and Information

The ability to interpret and absorb signals in the external environment is continually being reinforced – or confused – by a wide variety of signs such as public information signs, symbols and advertisements. Although they should aim to convey information in the most effective and simple manner, it is not uncommon to be faced with a clutter of confused and unsightly signs, in a variety of styles and materials, at different heights and orientations. Thoughtful selection and siting of signs can create visual order and help to convey information more coherently.

Siting

The number of signs should always be kept to a minimum. Wherever possible, signs should be mounted on other constructed elements, such as buildings, freestanding walls, fences and kiosks. Where several are required at a single location, it is helpful to mount them on one support as finger signs pointing towards a number of places or facilities, as used in hospitals or universities.

Illumination is essential for directional signs. They can be lit internally or by the pool of public lighting, to avoid the clutter of separate lighting units.

Materials

A wide range of materials and techniques is available. They include separately mounted letters; signs formed in iron, bronze, aluminium, ceramics and plastics; signs engraved on to stainless steel, bronze, aluminium and plastics, or carved into wood or stone. Complex monochrome or colour-separated artwork information can be reproduced on weather-resistant plastics, glass and enamel.

Durability varies enormously, so design decisions should take local circumstances into account. Glass or plastics may be fractured and scratched, metals may be bent and some, such as iron, steel or aluminium, can become unsightly by oxidizing, while enamel is vulnerable to chipping. Painted signs require regular repainting. Signs carved into stone can last for many decades if the stone is either built into a wall to prevent it from being damaged, or is a freestanding hard stone like granite.

Where local information is frequently changed, wall-mounted or freestanding display units with moisture-proof, transparent plastic or toughened glass, can be used with integral lighting. They can be grouped to form stable squares or triangles. The units may also be static or rotating drums. Vents, such as from

Figure 18.1   *Above:* The bold
advertisement punctuates low-level
planting in a contemporary industrial
location.

Figure 18.2   *Right:* A functional, but
visually pleasing, information signboard.

underground car parks or services, can then be concealed within them.

Design Selection

Factors to consider include mounting height, scale, materials, typeface and colours. The size and choice of typeface and the height of the sign related to the speed of movement of the user, and the relative important of the message in the street scene. Pictograms are easy to understand and so can be mounted higher and be smaller in scale than lettering.

Where many signs are required within a limited area, the sense of clutter can be reduced by the use of a coordinated range of uniform style and typeface, in a restricted colour range. Such a system will aid comprehension and good examples are demonstrated by the British Rail and BAA plc house styles.

Traffic Signs

Due to the difference in the speed of movement, there are two classes of signs – those for pedestrians (such as footpath waymarks) and those for motorists, which must be capable of being read at speed. Only the former are discussed here.

Commercial Signs

Good-quality, responsible advertising can make a positive contribution by bringing colour and even humour to an otherwise dismal, if orderly, urban scene. Nevertheless, however well designed it may be, the advertising should not dominate the visual environment. As the content will vary from time to time, the scale of the overall display should bear a sensitive relationship to its surroundings. Advertising can be incorporated readily into street furniture, such as kiosks, litter bins and bus shelters.

Control of Advertising

While advertisements can be regulated by 'The Town and Country Planning (Control of Advertisements) Regulations' 1984 (see Bibliography), a significant number of advertisements may be displayed without express consent. However, where the local planning authority legally defines 'Areas of Special Control' – for instance in Conservation Areas, National Parks and Areas of Outstanding Natural Beauty – it can use additional powers to regulate advertising. The local planning authority (under Schedule 1) ensures that all advertisements are kept in a clean and tidy condition and that hoardings are structurally sound.

Figure 18.3   Glazed ceramic tiles mounted in brickwork make an attractive alternative to conventional street naming.

CHAPTER 19

Bollards

Bollards have been used for centuries to protect people, ancient trees, monuments and property from passing vehicles. On the quayside, special bollards are used to moor vessels. The durability of traditional materials like granite, cast iron, elm and oak has ensured that many bollards that predate this century are still in use today.

Siting

Bollards can:

1. Protect pedestrians from traffic, while allowing both to circulate freely, by preventing vehicles encroaching on spaces reserved for people on foot – for example, by cutting corners or parking on footways, or by preventing vehicles entering alleyways or public passageways through or between buildings.
2. Allow service vehicles into pedestrianized areas in emergencies or at specific times, by using bollards which are collapsible or removable.
3. Prevent drivers from going on to uneven or soft ground. Bollards for this purpose should be close-spaced and at least 700mm high, so that they remain visible above snow. To be visible against snow, and at night, they require both dark and reflective finishes.
4. Warn pedestrians or cyclists of a potential hazard – for example, where a pathway discharges onto a road. However, short lengths of railing are a preferable alternative to bollards in this situation.
5. Protect exposed corners of buildings, trees, sculptures, monuments and low planting or grass from vehicle damage.
6. Mark boundaries and define zones, as in markets. In this context, bollards may require 'eyes' or some other means of attaching removable ropes or chains.
7. Provide low-level amenity lighting. Lighting can be incorporated into bollards used to define routes or boundaries.
8. Provide informal seating. Low, broad bollards are best for this purpose.
9. Be used for mooring boats, for which purpose bollards are shaped to retain ropes and need to be securely anchored.

To prevent vehicles passing at right angles between bollards, the gaps should be less than about 1.30m. Bollards alongside a highway, where traffic moves freely, may be spaced at about 4.00m intervals.

Bollards in turn require protection from heavy vehicles. They should be set at least 600mm back from the kerb edge and need to be arranged in a distinct line so that their purpose cannot be mistaken by drivers or pedestrians.

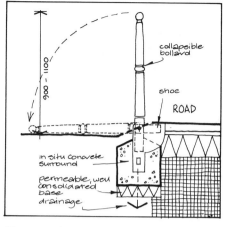

Figure 19.1   *Above:* Collapsible metal bollard detail.

Figure 19.2   *Right:* Short lengths of railing are more effective than bollards for restraining children or cyclists where a pathway discharges onto a road.

Figure 19.3   *Below:* A bollard can protect an exposed corner of a building.

Figure 19.4 *Above:* Cast iron bollards used for mooring ships and low stone bollards which double as informal seats.

Figure 19.5 *Right:* A sturdy timber bollard protects pedestrians and doubles as a traffic sign.

Materials and Construction

Natural stone, cast iron and timber bollards are widely used. Cast iron traditional designs are still manufactured and are gaining in popularity. These are particularly useful for urban rehabilitation projects, where design in harmony with the surrounding street landscape is particularly desirable. Existing bollards can be exactly copied in cast metal or carved stone. Precast concrete, glass reinforced concrete, steel aluminium and plastic bollards are also available.

When selecting bollards it is important to consider how resistant to damage the various materials are in relation to their intended function. Large-diameter, precast concrete bollards with substantial reinforcement, or concrete-filled steel tubes can resist all but the severest impact, but slender designs in concrete with light reinforcement are easily broken. Hardwoods, used in generous sizes, can absorb heavy impact with little significant damage to the bollard but softwoods are more vulnerable. Cast iron, while unsurpassed for elegance, is somewhat brittle.

Since the function of most bollards renders them liable to knocks and bumps, their surface treatment should be chosen to minimize maintenance. Particular attention should be paid to the specification of painted surfaces, as these can be chipped and soon look worn. For metal bollards, powder-coated finishes are more durable. For timber bollards, deep penetrating stains disguise defects and damage. Timber which has been pressure-impregnated with preservative should need no further treatment.

Adequate foundations are essential to prevent overturning or removal of bollards. Sufficient space above the foundation is necessary to allow for the paving material to be taken right up to the bollard. The foundations and sockets for removable or collapsible bollards must be installed in the paved area before the paving surface is laid.

For illuminated bollards, the linking underground cable ducts must be placed prior to other construction, and at sufficient depth to allow for planting of nearby trees or shrubs.

Maintenance

Fixed bollards require little maintenance, except repainting, unless they are knocked over. Illuminated bollards and removable fittings require a greater management input and their maintenance costs are consequently higher.

Figure 19.6   The spacing of bollards around pedestrian zones must be wide enough to allow wheelchairs to pass.

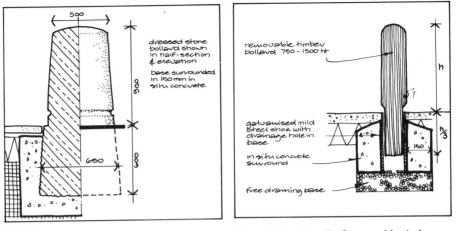

Figure 19.7   Stone bollard detail.

Figure 19.8   Detail of removable timber bollard.

Figure 19.9   Concrete bollards used to control parking in a narrow street.

CHAPTER 20

Litter Bins

Siting

Unlike almost any other item of furniture, litter bins need to be immediately obvious. They should be conveniently positioned close to where people sit and where they walk frequently – for example, at pathway intersections. On narrow footways, bins are best sited in recesses in walls or fencing, to avoid obstruction. Around paved spaces they can be set back into planting, with sufficient hard paving around them to allow easy sweeping up of dropped litter. They can also be mounted on buildings, kiosks and lamp posts to minimize unnecessary clutter in the street scene.

Design

The function of public litter bins is to encourage people to deposit their casual litter, including the remains of take-away meals, which attract vermin. Public litter bins and their internal wire baskets must be durable, relatively maintenance-free and have adequate drainage. The opening height should suit both adults and children and make litter collection easy. If bin openings are unduly wide, they may be used for bulky domestic or commercial refuse, which defeats their main purpose.

Bins should be selected to suit the location and to relate to other items of landscape furniture. In busy urban areas, only heavy precast or *in situ* concrete containers, with heavy steel fittings, or enclosures built up in brick, perhaps as part of a raised planting bed, are likely to be resistant to fire damage and vandalism. Bins of plastic, most coated metal finishes and timber are more appropriate in less intensively used areas. Bin capacity should meet anticipated demand and maintenance frequency.

Materials and Construction

A wide range of litter bins is available, made from wood, plastic, aluminium, stainless, enamelled or galvanized steel, wire mesh, precast concrete and glass reinforced concrete. Bins may also be built *in situ* from stone, brick, timber or concrete. Ready-made bins can be selected from manufacturers' ranges of landscape furniture to coordinate with planters, seats or bollards used elsewhere in the design.

Most bins are now constructed with a fixed outer casing or cladding which forms the structure, together with an inner, corrosion-resistant, lockable lining of perforated sheet metal or mesh, which can be removed for emptying. Alternatively, lightweight mesh bins can be locked on to fixed posts and released for emptying, but the litter is visible. Bins can be freestanding, secured to concrete pads, set into paving or fixed on to walls or buildings by non-corroding bolts. In isolated positions, bins should be sufficiently heavy to avoid being overturned.

Maintenance

There are three aspects to the management of litter collection from public places: the regular clearing of the waste; the routine inspection of the bin structure; and general sweeping.

Where maintenance vehicles are used for bin servicing, paved areas must be sufficiently wide and strong to take their weight without being damaged. Where emptying is infrequent, a hinged cover is essential to prevent rain from wetting the rubbish. Removable liners or plastic sacks should be limited in volume, so that the weight can be easily lifted by an average person, and be of good quality so that when full of refuse they do not split. In rural areas a hinged cover is required to prevent animals removing the contents.

The adoption of one style of fitting helps to simplify maintenance and ensures that litter bins are easily recognized by the general public.

Figure 20.1   There is still much scope for good design of litterbins. This is a prototype which may be specially manufactured for a large development.

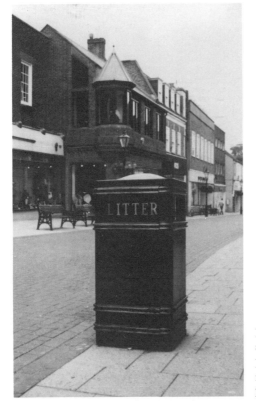

Figure 20.2 *Left:* Large bold litter bins are appropriate for pedestrian precincts.

Figure 20.3 *Below:* Less visible wall mounted litter bins may be suited to popular visitor locations like this quay.

CHAPTER 21

Lighting: The Night Landscape

This chapter introduces the broad principles of external lighting, a sometimes neglected aspect of landscape design. Street lighting for traffic safety is excluded, as is security lighting for industry and commerce, since they are both highly specialized fields.

The Quality of Light

To design with light, certain characteristics, espcially glare, shadow and colour rendering, should be carefully considered.

Glare

Sunlight reflected from light-coloured or shiny reflective surfaces causes glare. By night, concentrated lighting reflected from surfaces like glazed facades or wet roads also produces glare. On roads, it is made worse by repetitious movement – for example, car headlights passing an avenue of trees. Glare, which can produce momentary blindness and is potentially dangerous, can be reduced by screening the source of light – for example, by planting a hedge along the central reservation of a dual carriageway, by increasing background light levels, or by altering the angle and direction of fixed light sources.

Shadows

Shadows can be defined in terms of degree of shade, ranging from unlit areas through partial shadow to lightly shaded surfaces. Once an area has been reserved purely for people on foot, shadows can be consciously used as a design technique to enliven an entire scheme, by emphasizing its three-dimensional form. This can be further developed by highlighting the contrast with the subtle use of floodlighting. Similarly, silhouette or backlighting can be used to make selected elements in the scene stand out dramatically, although glare should not be allowed to cause discomfort for people approaching the light source.

Colour rendering

This is the ability of a light source to reveal the natural daylight colours of a scene or an object. It is a most important factor, as it can enhance or diminish the quality of the intended environmental experience. If lighting is poorly designed with inappropriate lamps, information on colour-coded direction signs, for instance, may be ineffective and the colour of vegetation may be reduced to depressing shades of yellow or black.

Some lamps, for instance, low-pressure sodium vapour, give very poor colour rendering. Although the eye does eventually adapt, the process is slow. Under such lighting conditions, people unfamiliar with the landscape may have difficulty in even perceiving forms at night.

Product Design

Coordinated lighting systems are available as a range of fittings for a variety of function, the use of which can give unity to a scheme and greatly simplify maintenance. Coherent design is essential. For example, it is preferable to use one type of lighting column with single fittings or with multiple fittings to give more light where needed, rather than using an assortment of lighting fittings. The scale of lighting systems should also be considered in the context of their contribution to design harmony in the daytime.

Light fittings consist of three basic parts:

a)   the lamp – that is, the light source;
b)   the luminaire – that is, the lamp housing, incorporating the electrical supply providing weatherproofing and protection to the lamp;

Figure 21.1 *Pictures above and opposite:* The use of a coordinated range of light fittings for a variety of functions can give unity to a scheme.

c)   the supporting structure, either column or bracket.

Lamps can be assessed in terms of four characteristics:

1.   type of light source – that is, the discharge or filament;
2.   efficiency of light source – that is, the relationship between light output and power input;
3.   light output in terms of quality and appearance, including colour;
4.   the effect of the light upon the object to be observed – that is, its colour rendering.

Lamps

Lamps should be selected carefully from the main types set out in Table 21.1 below.

Table 21.1   Lamp types

LAMP TYPES*			LIFE (hours)
	Filament Lamps i.e. Tungsten Filament in Halogen or other inert gas		1–2,000hrs
Discharge Lamps	Tubular Fluorescent		2,000 plus
		High pressure Sodium	7–8,000
		Low pressure Sodium	
		High pressure Mercury	
		High pressure Mercury blended	
		Metal Halide	

*See the Lighting Industry Federation, *Lamp Guide*.

Filament lamps These are often used for low output applications or for local or point lighting. They give good colour rendering because of their wide band output across the visible spectrum.

Discharge lamps These are used where the quantity of output is paramount, at the expense of quality. All types of discharge lamps have narrow band outputs and are monochromatic. The quality of the light of discharge lamps may be improved by the mixing of the types of phosphate coating on the bulb. The incorporation of different types of inert gases in the bulb also modifies the output colour.

The Luminaire

The luminaire establishes the physical appearance of the lamp fitting. In terms of size, materials and shape it is an important design element. The shape of the beam of light can be controlled by reflectors behind the lamp, by refractors, or by diffusers in front.

Luminaires should be made of sturdy materials with minimal corrosion risks and good life expectancy. In public areas, impact-resistant materials, such as acrylic and polycarbonates, should be used rather than glass. Where vandalism is anticipated, fittings should be relatively inaccessible and floodlighting or recessed wall fittings may be considered.

The Supporting Structure

The supporting structure is the column, or bracket which supports the luminaire at the correct height to give the required spread of light. Columns may be either bolted down to a foundation, or cast into a concrete base. Luminaires may also be fixed to walls with brackets or recessed into the wall itself.

Posts are available in a variety of materials including being prefabricated in aluminium, cast iron, galvanized steel or reinforced plastics. Brackets, columns and luminaires should be considered as an integral design and should relate to other items of landscape furniture.

Design Opportunities

There are four main types of outdoor lighting applications:
a)   lighting to provide a general level of illumination over a wide area;

Figure 21.2   A neat, low-level light fitting can help pedestrians to interpret the scene safely.

b)   local lighting – for instance, to illustrate part of an area where a high level of light for a specific purpose such as at an entrance gate;

c)   floodlighting to provide a high level of illumination over a large area – for example, to illuminate the facade of a building;

d)   point floodlighting to provide highlighting for a special feature such as a piece of sculpture or a fountain.

Some of the more important ways in which these can be used are considered briefly below.

Lighting for Pedestrians

Lighting can help pedestrians to interpret the scene safely by drawing attention to specific features liable to cause people to falter or trip. These may include steps, kerbs, ramps, low walls, road crossings, entrances, and other potentially hazardous features.

In public areas, parks or gardens which are open at night, good lighting helps to deter potential aggressors and allow people to feel confident about using such areas after dark. Higher light levels are desirable where people pause, stop or enter a park.

However, it can be counterproductive to illuminate the main pathways brightly, as this may cause the surroundings to appear enveloped in darkness. In other words, an area approach to lighting design should be considered, rather than a strictly linear one linking the major entrances or activity areas together.

As well as making the night safer for pedestrians and providing a sense of security, lighting can enhance the pleasure of an evening walk. High-level or localized lighting can draw attention to focal points such as fine groups of trees, a fountain or a piece of sculpture.

Figure 21.3   Although lighting at low level does not provide extensive illumination, it can highlight key features and the sculptural quality of planting.

Lighting for Civic Spaces

Lighting design should consider the safety of pedestrians and the ability of motorists to follow vehicular routes. However, this can lead to a conflict of interests. Designs aimed at efficient vehicle movement encourage greater speeds and, due to high contrasts in lighting levels, pedestrian areas may be left dangerously underilluminated and in relative shadow, thus reducing the safety of those most in need of protection. Other measures to provide for the safety of pedestrians may also need to be considered in the overall design.

Physical subdivision to create different zones, efficiently lit, can create a safe and appropriate environment for both uses. A zone for pedestrians can be cheerfully lit with colour-true lamps and be separated from the traffic zone by broad, softly lit planting areas to reduce the contrast with the high intensity lighting necessary for vehicles. This concept could be applied to squares surrounded by traffic routes.

Car Parks

Good general lighting levels are required to ensure that drivers and pedestrian can see each other easily. It will also make it safer to cross the area at night and help drivers to find empty parking bays. It may also assist in security and supervision. Two levels of lighting are desirable; general overall area lighting from medium height columns, combined with low-level lighting from bollard or mushroom fittings amongst low planting, to ensure that kerbs or steps are well lit to assist people arriving or leaving on foot.

Street Lighting

In narrow streets, fittings are less obtrusive if they can be mounted on the face of the buildings. Although supplementary lighting may be necessary to avoid 'dead' areas outside the 'throw' of wall-mounted fittings, there is a real gain in having a footway that is free from visual and physical clutter.

Lighting for Celebrations

Whenever a public celebration, exhibition or market takes place after dark, additional display lighting is usually needed. Lines of small filament lamps are frequently used because of their great adaptability. A tracery of these lamps criss-crossing over a busy space adds sparkle and appeal to the scene, especially when they are hung through the branches of trees.

Low-level Lighting

Lighting at low level, provided by fittings close to the ground, or by illuminated bollards, is not an efficient method of providing extensive illumination. However, it can be used to improve significantly the visual quality of the night landscape by highlighting key features such as steps, archways, fountains, sculptures, enclosing walls and the sculptural quality of planting. Low-level lighting also helps to identify possible hazards like water features. Low-level fittings are significantly more vulnerable to vandalism and so only the most robust and secure types should be chosen.

Illuminating Planting

Foliage and flowers require good colour rendering, preferably from tungsten filament or tungsten halogen lamps. Trees should be illuminated selectively – for example, particularly attractive or grand specimens at focal points. Their foliage can appear dramatic when illuminated from below using fittings recessed in the ground. Alternatively, small floodlights amongst the branches can give local or general light to the whole tree canopy. Even in winter, the bare branches of a group of mature trees can be most attractive when well lit. Silhouette or backlighting may give the best results with a particularly attractive tree form or beautiful branch tracery, often found in trees such as the plane, beech, oak, acacia, walnut or low, broad spreading trees like the mulberry.

Lighting Water

Attractive designs can be formed by using light in relation to water. The possibilities are endless – they may be stimulating, calm or brilliant. Superb reflections can be obtained from still water using floodlighting. But viewpoints, water areas and scenes to be reflected must all be correctly interrelated, both in space and in scale, for this to be achieved successfully.

At night, moving water can be just as exciting as it is in the day, if properly illuminated. Submersible luminaires can even direct light rays along water jets or streams. Fountains or waterfalls can be lit internally from one side, or with hidden 'backlighting' to produce a scintillating water curtain. Further technical possibilities include automatic dimming, colour sequences and complementary turbulence and water jet patterns, used to create exciting programmed displays. However, it is advisable to contact a consultant or a specialist manufacturer in view of the considerable technical complexities.

Legal Constraints

Under town and country planning legislation, works carried out adjacent to a public highway boundary may require design approval of the local authority. Similarly, prior consent is necessary if fittings are to be attached to the fabric of scheduled monuments or listed buildings. Special considerations apply to lighting near railways, airports or navigable waterways. Finally, electrical installations must conform with the general conditions and safety regulations of the local electricity board and with the current regulations of the Institute of Electrical Engineers. In each case, the appropriate authority must be consulted at the earliest stage.

Maintenance

Maintenance consists of regular cleaning and lamp replacement. The frequency will depend on the type of lamp and the degree of pollution, accidental damage and vandalism. For small-scale lighting, maintenance is carried out from the ground with the assistance of an elevating platform where required. For taller installations, some columns are hinged so that the luminaire can be raised and lowered for maintenance. For safety, the hinge should be strong and also should not interfere with the smooth lines of the column. The necessary control gear should be housed in the base.

Figure 21.4 A dramatic night-time backcloth for a public open space can be created by skilfully floodlit water and planting.

Bibliography

This bibliography has been prepared by Christine Smith of The Property Services Agency Library Services. As far as information was available, it was up to date as at February 1990. This bibliography does not claim to be a definitive list of all books available on Landscape Design, but gives a selection of those which might prove useful. Most of the publications cited are available in the United Kingdom.

Please note British Standards are listed at the end.

Allotments

Crouche, D. and Ward, C. (1988) *The Allotment: its landscape and culture.* London: Faber.

Bioengineering

Bache, D.H. and MacAskill, I.A. (eds) (1984) *Vegetation in civil and landscape engineering.* London: Granada. 317pp. (ISBN 0246115076).

Demonstrates the wide range of applications for vegetation as an engineering medium and evaluates its role in environmental control.

Stiles, R. (1988) 'Engineering with vegetation', *Landscape Design,* April, pp. 57–61.

Stresses the importance of the hitherto neglected science of bioengineering in the landscape.

Conservation

Conservation monitoring the management (1987) Cheltenham, Glos.: Countryside Commission.

Dodd, J. (1985) 'Landscape development for energy saving', *Construction,* vol. 52, Autumn, pp. 6–11.

Shows how the provision of well-designed external shelter can make the development site climate increase comfort, reduce wind damage and make worthwhile energy savings.

Poore, D. and J. (1987) *Protected Landscapes: the United Kingdom experience.* Cheltenham, Glos.: Countryside Commission.

Putwain, P.D. and Gillham, D.A. (1988) 'Restoration of heather moorland', *Landscape Design,* April, pp. 51–6.

Explains a seven-year experiment to restore heather moorland destroyed by china-clay waste heaps.

Disabled

Goldsmith, S. (1984, updated edn) *Designing for the disabled*. RIBA Publications. 525pp. (ISBN 0900630507).

Gives anthropometric and measurement information, building elements and finishes, services, installations, general spaces, public buildings and housing.

Thorpe, Stephen (1986) *Designing for people with sensory impairments*. Centre on Environment for the Handicapped. 21pp. (ISBN 090397617).

Aims to provide guidance for designers of public buildings and spaces for people with sensory impairments. Also for planning outdoor spaces, new building design, and adaptation of existing buildings, and to assist all those whose work affects the quality of the built environment to go beyond meeting statutory obligations and respond to the needs of people with sensory impairments.

Ecology

Johnston, M. (1983) 'Urban trees and an ecological approach to urban landscape design', *Arboricultural Journal*, November, pp. 275–82.

Madders, M. and Laurence, M. (1981) 'Air pollution control by vegetation buffer zones', *Landscape Design*, August, pp. 29–31.

McHarg, I.L. (1969) *Design with nature*. New York: Natural History Press.

Provides an ecological viewpoint to the design of landscape in urban and rural areas.

Fences

see also Hedges, Shelterbelts, Walls and BS 1722

British Trust for Conservation Volunteers (1986) *Fencing: a practical conservation handbook*. Wallingford 141 pp. (ISBN 0946752044).

Practical, comprehensive information is provided for design and siting, safety, strained fencing (materials and construction), wooden and electric fencing and gates and stiles.

Central Electricity Generating Board (1965) *Design memorandum on the use of fences*. 36pp.

Diagrams illustrate the use of fences, barriers, walls and hedges which form important visual effects in a landscape.

Jaffa, G. (1985) 'Fencing requirements in the eyes of the law', *Parks and Sports Grounds*, January, pp. 10–11.

Historic boundaries, maintenance rights.

Pepper, H.Q. and Tee, L.A. (1986) *Forest fencing*. 2nd edn. London: HMSO, Forestry Commission Leaflet no. 87. 42pp.

Discusses fence components and associated tools, fence construction and maintenance, and the principles and specification for fencing.

Follies and Pavilions

Headley, B. and Meulenkamp, W. (1986) *Follies: A National Trust Guide.* London: Jonathan Cape. xxviii. 564pp (ISBN 0224021052).

Describes structures erected in complete disregard for building practices, or tastes, on impossible sites with no easy access, with costs out of proportion to their use. These structures may well add interest to the landscape.

Jones, B. (1974) *Follies and grottoes.* London: Constable. 459pp. (ISBN 0094593507).

Describes follies and grottoes and shows how they may enhance a landscape.

Smith, J. Abel (1978) *Pavilions in peril.* Ed. by Sophie Andreae. SAVE Britain's Heritage. 40pp. (ISBN 0905978234).

Considers various garden accessories in danger – pavilions, gazebos, grottoes, garden buildings of various types. Also describes the gardens and historic houses and grounds where these items may be located.

Footbridges

Footbridges in the Countryside: design and construction (1981) Perth: Countryside Commission for Scotland. 101pp. (ISBN 0902226525).

Illustrates in detail aspects of footbridge selection, design, construction and maintenance.

Forestry

see also Trees and Woodland

Campbell, D. (1987) 'Landscape design in forestry', *Landscape Design,* April, pp. 31–3, 35–6.

The Forestry Commission's landscape architects reflect on the development of their landscape policy over the past twenty-five years.

Forestry in the Countryside (1987) Cheltenham, Glos.: Countryside Commission. CCP 245. (ISBN 0861701976).

Describes the role the Commission thinks forestry should play in the countryside. It makes a number of recommendations for action by government and other agencies and outlines a number of initiatives which the Commission proposes to take.

Garden Design

Brookes, J. (1979) *Room outside: a new approach to garden design.* London: Thames and Hudson. 256pp. (ISBN 0500271372).

Covers design, ground shaping and drainage, enclosure, hard surfacing, soft ground surfacing, skeleton planting, planting design, garden furnishings, special features such as water, rockeries.

Brookes, J. (1989) *The new small garden book*. London: Dorling Kindersley Limited. 224pp. (ISBN 0863183484).

A comprehensive look at the variety of designs possible for small areas and the use of plants.

Brown, J. (1986) *The English garden in our time from Gertrude Jekyll to Geoffrey Jellicoe*. Woodbridge, Suffolk: Antique Collectors Club. 272pp. (ISBN 1851490124).

Looks at twentieth-century garden design. Includes sections on the Arts and Crafts Movement, the Italian influence, the Modern Movement, 'New Georgian' gardens and the work of Sir Geoffrey Jellicoe.

Crowe, S. (1981) *Garden design*. Packard Publishing. 224pp. (ISBN 0906527058).

Presents a history of design in gardens and examines the need for these principles to be applied to the contemporary landscape.

Elliott, B. (1986) *Victorian gardens*. London: B.T. Batsford. 285pp. (ISBN 071344763X).

Victorian gardens resulted from rebellion against eighteenth century landscape parks. Gives the history of the Victorian gardening movement, creation of jobs, design, art and nature, conservatories, carpet bedding, the use of colour. Also remarks on Dutch, Italian and Old English gardens. Includes Edwardian gardens.

Jellicoe, G. and S. (eds) (1986) *The Oxford companion to gardens*. OUP. 651pp. (ISBN 0198661231).

Over 1500 entries embracing articles from history of garden design to short definitions of terms. Individual entries for 700 gardens – layout, special characteristics and significance. Biographical entries for designers, gardeners,plant collectors and garden enthusiasts.

Paul, A. and Rees, Y. (1988) *The garden design book*. London: Collins.

Selected garden designers consider their philosophy and reviews certain of their designs.

The Sunday Times (1983) *The making of the English garden*. London:Macmillan.

Titchmarsh, A. (1988) *The concise encyclopaedia of gardening techniques*. London: Mitchell Beazley.

Triggs, H.I. (1988) *Formal gardens in England and Scotland*. Woodbridge, Suffolk: Antique Collectors Club.

Turner, T. (1986) *English garden design: history and styles since 1650*. Woodbridge, Suffolk: Antique Collectors Club. 238pp. (ISBN 0907462251).

Covers the background ideas: the period 1650–1740 which discusses the enclosed French and Dutch styles; 1714–1810 includes the Forest, Serpentine and irregular styles; 1794–1870 covers the Transition, Italian and Mixed styles; 1870–1985 embraces the Arts and Crafts and Abstract styles and includes recent trends.

Greenbelts

Elson, M. (1986) *Green belts: conflict mediation in the urban fringe.* London: Heinemann. (ISBN 0434905321).

Planning for countryside in Metropolitan areas (1987) Cheltenham, Glos.: Countryside Commission.

Hedges

see also Fences, Shelterbelts and Walls

British Trust for Conservation Volunteers (1988) *Hedging: a practical conservation handbook.* Comp. by A. Brooks; 3rd rev. edn. by E. Agate. Wallingford, Oxford. 120pp. (ISBN 0946752628).

Deals with farm hedges, hedges with a practical purpose, and hedges which are stock fences or shelter plantings. Explains different methods of regional styles of hedge laying and discusses choice of plant species, planting and various methods of management.

Hedge management (1980) Cheltenham, Glos.: Countryside Commission. Leaflet no. 7. (ISBN 0902590977).

History of Landscape

Hoskins, W.G. (1988) *The making of the English landscape.* Sevenoaks, Kent: Hodder. (ISBN 0340399716).

Describes the English landscape through the ages.

Jellicoe, G. and S. (1987) *The landscape of man: Shaping the environment from prehistory to the present day.* London: Thames and Hudson. 400pp. (ISBN 0500274312).

A concise global view of the designed landscape past and present, with 734 illustrations.

Industrial Landscape

Crowe, S. (1958) *The landscape of power.* Architectural Press. 115pp.

Power stations, hydroelectric power, oil, airfields, power and national parks.

Tandy, C. (1975) *Landscape of industry.* New York/London: John Wiley. 314pp. (ISBN 047084440X).

Concerned with the impact of industry on the landscape in the past, the present and the future. Looks at the damage which has been done to the environment by industry and studies methods by which this damage can be rectified.

Land Classification

Landscape assessment of farmland (1988) Cheltenham, Glos.: Countryside Commission.

Tansley, Sir A.G. (1965) *The British Islands and their vegetation.* Cambridge: University Press. 2 vols. (ISBN 052106600X).

Chapters on the nature and classification of vegetation including woodland, grassland, fen, marsh and bog vegetation, heath and moor, and marine vegetation.

Land Reclamation

Bradshaw, A.D. and Chadwick, M.J. (1980) *The restoration of land.* Oxford: Blackwell. (ISBN 0632091800).

Deals with the problems of derelict land on a global scale and shows how the problems can be solved most effectively through a scientific understanding of the ecological factors which affect plant growth.

Cairney, T. (ed.) 1987) *Reclaiming contaminated land.* Glasgow: Blackie & Son Ltd. 272pp. (ISBN 021691874X).

Chapters cover: recognition of the problem; types of contaminated land; main types of contaminants; appropriate site investigations; available reclamation methods; soil cover reclamations; long-term monitoring of reclaimed sites; safety in site reclamation; policy planning and financial issues; landscaping and vegetating reclaimed sites; hazards from methane and carbon monoxide.

Land Use

The changing landscape (1988) Cheltenham, Glos.: Countryside Commission.

Landscape Institute (1985) *Farmed landscapes: A balanced future.* Landscape Institute. 32pp.

Advocates the creation by the government of a countryside register and management scheme in order to preserve a balance between conservation and the agricultural use of land.

New opportunities for the countryside (1987) Cheltenham, Glos.: Countryside Commission.

Stamp, L.D. (1962) *The land of Britain: its use and misuse.* 3rd edn. London: Longmans. 545pp.

Land use, soils, farming.

Landscape Architects

Harvey, S. (ed.) (1987) *Reflections on landscape: The lives and work of six British landscape architects.* Aldershot: Gower. 155pp. (ISBN 0291397085).

Based on interviews, this book includes chapters on: Sir Geoffrey Jellicoe, Dame Sylvia Crowe, Sir Peter Shepheard, Brian Hackett, Peter Youngman and Brenda Colvin.

Landscape Design

see also BS 1192 : Part 4, BS 4428

Aldous, T. and Clouston, B. (1979) *Landscape by design.* London: Heinemann. 173pp. O/P (ISBN 0434018058).

Outlines the development of the landscape profession in Great Britain since the foundation of the Landscape Institute in 1929. The background, aims and results of main landscape schemes for new towns, industry and local authorities are discussed.

Alpern, A. (1982) *Handbook of speciality elements in architecture.* Maidenhead, Berks: McGraw-Hill. 484pp. (ISBN 0070013608).

Deals with the special features that make buildings both functionally and aesthetically distinctive: exterior lighting; interior and exterior trees and plants; works of art; pools and fountains; signage; audiovisual communications; and accommodation for the disabled.

Austin, R.L. (1984) *Designing the natural landscape.* London: Van Nostrand Reinhold. 117pp. (ISBN 0442209789).

A practical sourcebook providing specifications for planting trees, shrubs and vines, design criteria for water features, standards and specifications for the development of wildlife habitats and case studies of individual landscape projects.

Booth, N.K. (1983) *Basic elements of landscape architectural design.* Barking, Essex: Elsevier. 315pp. (ISBN 0444007660).

Considers the significance and potential uses of landform, plant materials, buildings, pavement, site structures and water in landscape architecture.

Colvin, B. (1970) *Land and landscape: evolution design and control.* 2nd edn. London: John Murray. 414pp. O/P (ISBN 0719518008).

Covers landscape development, principles and practice of design.

Evans, B.M. (ed.) 1984) *Proceedings of the 'Greenchips' symposium on computer-aided landscape design: Principles and practice,* University of Strathclyde, 1983. Scotland: Landscape Institute. 165pp. (ISBN 0950961302).

Fairbrother, N. (1974) *The nature of landscape design.* New York: Alfred A. Knopf. 252pp. (ISBN 039447046X).

Hannebaum, L. (1981) *Landscape design: A practical approach.* Reston Publishing Company. 392pp. (ISBN 0835939340).

Provides information on landscape design, the study of land forms, environmental design, drainage of surface and subsurface water and retaining wall design.

Ingels, J.E. (1983) *The landscape book.* 2nd edn. London: Van Nostrand Reinhold. 273pp. (ISBN 0442242174).

Practical information on the basic principles of landscape design, construction, materials and maintenance.

Landphair, H.C. and Klatt, F. (1988) *Landscape architecture construction.* Barking, Essex: Elsevier. 433pp. (ISBN 0444012869).

Emphasizes the creative use of technology through an awareness of the alternatives among available tools and construction processes.

Laurie, M. (1986) *An introduction to landscape architecture.* 2nd edn. Barking, Essex: Elsevier. 248pp. (ISBN 044409701)

Deals with various aspects of landscape architecture and how it has developed over recent years. Covers ecological analysis, conservation and landscape planning.

Simonds, J.O. (1983) *Landscape architecture: A manual of site planning and design.* New York: McGraw-Hill. 331pp. (ISBN 0070574480).

Information on site, visual aspects of plan arrangement and structures in the landscape.

Tregay, R. and Gustavsson, R. (1983) *Oakwood's new landscape: Designing for nature in the residential environment.* Warrington and Runcorn Development Corporation. (ISBN 9157614504).

Oakwood's new landscape is seen as one of the most thorough examples of an ecological approach to landscape development in England. Describes the main principles and ideas during the construction period.

Weddle, A.E. (1979) *Landscape techniques.* London: Heinemann. 265pp. (ISBN 0434922277).

Describes the range of techniques that can be used by the landscape architect. Covers conservation and management of the coastline, ground modelling, trees and planting, turf, maintenance practices.

Landscape Planning

see also Conservation

Dodd. J. (1989) 'Greenscape', *Architects Journal,* April–May.

Hackett, B. (1971) *Landscape planning: an introduction to theory and practice.* Oriel Press. 124pp. (ISBN 0853621209).

Landscape planning techniques, ecology, aesthetics, conservation and recreation.

Jacobs, J. (1977) *Death and life of great American cities.* Harmondsworth: Penguin Books. 474pp. (ISBN 0140206817).

Deals with failures in town planning – good ideas that went wrong.

Lynch, K. and Hack, G. (1984) *Site planning.* 3rd edn. Cambridge, Mass./London: MIT Press. 499pp. (ISBN 0262121069).

The introductory chapter summarizes the site planning process and subsequent chapters provide a case study of a typical project covering such topics as user analysis, programming, design strategies, mapping and environmental impact analysis.

Turner, T. (1987) *Landscape planning*. London: Hutchinson. 213pp. (ISBN 009164710X).

Covers landscape theory and landscape of industry, reservoirs, mines, quarries, parks, forestry, flood control, housing, new towns, and the renewal of the urban landscape.

Landscape Practice

Clamp, H. (1988) *The shorter forms of building contract*. 2nd edn. Oxford: BSP Professional Books. 170pp. (ISBN 0632018437).

Concentrates on the 1980 JCT Form of Building Agreement for Minor Works but also surveys a range of other shorter forms.

Clamp, H. (ed.) (1986) *Spon's landscape contract manual: A guide to good practice and procedures in the management of landscape contracts*. London: Spon. 195pp. (ISBN 0419134808).

Lovejoy, D. & Partners (eds.) (1986) *SPON's Landscape handbook*. 3rd edn. London: Spon. 470pp. (ISBN 0419133801).

Covers fees; town planning; site investigations; use of trees; data collection and landscape drawings; computer-aided design and information technology; specifications for siteworks; soft landscape works; hard landscape works; sports and recreation; water features; street and garden furniture; mechanical plant. Includes bibliography, list of manufacturers and suppliers.

Lovejoy, D. & Partners (eds.) (annual) *SPON's Landscape and external works price book*. London: Spon.

Covers all items needed for a medium-sized hard and soft landscape contract; recent legislation, fees and preliminaries, prices for measured work, approximate estimates.

Legislation

Harte, J.D.C. (1985) *Landscape, land use and the law*. London: Spon. 450pp. (ISBN 0419125108).

Provides comprehensive treatment of land boundaries, legal arrangements for controlling the use of land and legal responsibilities.

Heap, D. (1987) *Outline of planning law*. 9th edn. London: Sweet & Maxwell. (ISBN 0421354402).

Focuses on plans and control of development, public enquiries.

Lighting

see also BS 873

Bell, J. (1987) 'Lighting the landscape', *Landscape Design,* December, pp.58–60.

Describes what to look for in lighting projects.

Caminada, J.F. (1987) 'Lighting in residential areas', *Landscape Design*, December, pp.61–5.

Places emphasis on the safety and social aspects of residential lighting.

Cassidy, D. (1988) 'Shedding some light ...', *Landscape Design*, April, pp. 40–4.

Use of lighting in landscape design.

Dodds, B. 'Lighting design – and art form', *Landscape Design*, February, pp. 50–2.

Describes the importance of site-specific lighting, quoting the unusual example of the Queen Elizabeth Hospital, Alberta, Canada.

Electricity Council (1983) *Outdoor lighting.* Electricity Council. 36pp.

Sets out to encourage the effective and imaginative use of exterior lighting, with due regard to the wise use of energy. It considers building floodlighting, sports lighting, security lighting, and advertising.

Harvey, S. (comp.) (1988) 'Lighting bibliography', *Landscape Design*, April, p.45.

Lighting Industry Federation (1980) *Lamp guide.* London: Lighting Industry Federation. 11pp.

Reviews the basic types of lamp and explains their different characteristics.

Lovejoy, D. (1988) 'Light on the roads', *Landscape Design*, February, pp.53–6.

Considers the special problems associated with lighting motorways and major roads.

Open Spaces

Lambert, C.M. (comp.) (1981) *Urban open spaces: A select list of material based on the DOE/DTp library.* Department of the Environment. Library Bibliography no. 956. 52pp. (ISBN 0718401824).

Parks

Design Council (1979) *Equipment for parks and amenity areas.* Design Council. 114pp. (ISBN 0850720834).

A catalogue of equipment for parks and amenity areas that have been chosen by the Council's Street Furniture Advisory Committee for their high standard of design.

Wright, T. (1982) *Large gardens and parks, maintenance, management and design.* London: Granada. 194pp. (ISBN 0246114029).

Covers contemporary garden management, design, restoration of neglected or abandoned gardens and maintenance of historic gardens.

Paving – General

see also Pedestrian Areas and BS 340, BS 6677

Beazley, E. (1960) *Design and detail of the space between buildings.* Architectural Press. 230pp.

Includes paved spaces, trim of paved spaces, walls and fences and planning.

Bolton, H. (1988) 'Setting the street in Norwich', *Landscape Design,* October, pp.27–31.

Describes the details of paving and design in the revitalized pedestrian scheme in Norwich city centre.

Department of the Environment (1970) *A guide to the structural design of pavements for new roads.* Third edn. London: HMSO. 36pp. Road Research Laboratory: Road Note 29. O/P. (ISBN 0115501584).

Guide to hard landscape. (1986) Architects Journal Supplement 26 November.

Sponsored by the Brick Development Association (BDA), the supplement deals with reworking existing town centre developments; promoting new schemes such as science parks where landscape is an important factor. Includes lighting landscape; use of blocks and pavers; freestanding and retaining walls.

Howcroft, H. (1988) 'The techniques of sett laying', *Landscape Design,* October, pp.46–9.

Provides basic guidelines.

National Paving and Kerb Association (1984) *Paving flags: The product selector: to BS 368.* Folder.

Leaflets entitled: Techniques for laying; Small element paving flags, paving for the blind.

Scottish Local Authorities Special Housing Group (1975) *External environment. Hard surfaces: edging.* Edinburgh: SLASH Research Unit. pag. var.

Covers design, materials and their properties, bonding patterns, component drawings and standard details and preambles.

Tandy, C. (ed.) (1978) *Handbook of urban landscape.* Architectural Press. Paperback edn. First published 1972. 275pp. (ISBN 0851396917).

Section 10 'Elements of landscape construction' includes information sheets on surface treatments and pavings.

Paving – Brick

see also BS 187, BS 3921

Brick Development Association (1984) *Brick pavements.* 11pp.

Illustrated guide to the design and construction of flexible brick pavements.

Hammett, M. (1988) 'A new look at an old material', *Landscape Design*, October, pp. 39–43.

Reviews present practice and use of brick in the design of paving and walls.

Handisyde, C. (1976) *Hard landscape in brick*. Architectural Press. 72pp. (ISBN 0851392830).

Detailed, illustrated guidance on the use of brick for paving and as a landscape material.

Paving – Clay and Calcium Silicate

see also BS 6677

Brick Development Association (1988) *Specification for clay pavers for flexible pavements*. Brick Development Association with the co-operation of the County Surveyors' Society. 8pp.

Cook, I.D. (1981) *Flexible clay and calcium silicate paving for lightly trafficked roads and paved areas*. Brick Development Association. Design Note: no. 5. 8pp.

Contains design guidance and practical laying recommendations for flexible pavements of clay and calcium silicate. Applies to the design of lightly trafficked pavements intended to carry no more than 1.5 million standard (8200 kg) axles during their design lives.

Hammett, M. and Smith, R.A. (1984) *Rigid paving with clay and calcium silicate*. Brick Development Association. 15pp.

Deals mainly with paving out-of-doors and covers the laying of pavers on a mortar bed and with a mortar joint between each joint.

Smith, R. (1988) *Code of practice for flexible pavements constructed in clay pavers*. Brick Development Association. 8pp.

Smith, R.A. (1985) *Flexible paving with clay and calcium silicate pavers*. Brick Development Association. 32pp.

Paving – Cobble

Downing, M.F. (1977) *Landscape construction*. London: Spon. 247pp. (ISBN 0419108904).

Use of cobbles as a paving material given in pages 152–3.

Howarth, M. (1988) 'The art of cobblestones', *Landscape Design*, October, pp. 34–7.

Calls for a new look at an old tradition and shows some of the exciting modern cobblestone designs.

Paving – Concrete

see also BS 6717

Cement and Concrete Association (1983) *Code of practice for laying precast concrete paving blocks.* Cement and Concrete Association: County Surveyors Society and Interlocking Paving Association (Interpave). 7pp. (ISBN 072101285X).

Duell, J. (1981) 'Products in practice: External paving – product selection and specification', *Architects Journal*, vol. 173, no. 18, 6 May, pp.861–9.

Compares different types of concrete and clay units for jointed external paving. Provides information on sizes, patterns and gives notes on the detailing and installation.

Lilley, A.A. and Collins, J.R. (1984) *Laying concrete block paving.* Cement and Concrete Association. 15pp.

Maynard, D.M. (1983) *In situ concrete for industrial paving.* Cement and Concrete Association. Design Guide. 7pp. (ISBN 0721013007).

The design guide is for engineers, architects and contractors concerned with the design, supervision and construction of concrete paving for external industrial uses.

Pritchard, C. (1988) 'Concrete block paving', *Landscape Design*, October, pp. 50–3.

Describes quality, uses, design and layout.

Paving – Mastic Asphalt

Mastic Asphalt Council and Employers Federation (1980) *Paving handbook.* 20pp.

Provides guidance on the use of mastic asphalt in a variety of paving applications.

Paving – Stone

Booth, N.K. (1983) *Basic elements of landscape architectural design.* Barking, Essex: Elsevier. 315pp. (ISBN 0444007660).

Considers the significance and potential uses of landform, plant materials, buildings, pavements, site structures and water in landscape architecture. Pages 190–4 deal with stone setts.

Natural Stone Directory 1985: Dimension stone sources for Britain and Ireland/ Stone Industries. (1985) Ealing Publications. 124pp.

Includes sections on durability assessment, the stone of Britain, index to UK and Irish active quarries, stones grouped by colour, stone tracer (materials now unavailable), materials source guide, masonry training facilities.

Pedestrian Areas

see also Paving, Urban Landscape

Morgan, N. (1988) 'Pedestrianised zones in urban areas', *Landscape Design*, October, pp.24–6.

A case study reveals the influence of landscape architects and calls for greater imagination and creativity.

Plant Selection

see also BS 3975

Brickell, C.B. (ed.) (1980) *International code of nomenclature for cultivated plants.* Bohn, Scheltema, Holkema, Utrecht, The Netherlands. Regnum Vegetabilae, vol. 104. 32pp. (ISBN 9031304468).

Ferguson, N. (1984) *Garden plant directory: the essential guide to planning your garden.* London: Pan Books. 292pp. (ISBN 0330265946).

Illustrates more than 1400 plants and for each plant gives botanical and common name, height, flowering season, flower colour, important and individual characteristics.

Grouter, W. (ed.) (1988) *International code of botanical nomenclature.* Federal Republic of Germany: Koelz Scientific Books. i-xiv. Regnum Vegetabilae Series. 328pp. (ISBN 3874292789).

Joint Liaison Committee on Plant Supplies (1981) *Herbaceous plants: exotic and British native.* Horticultural Trades Association. 28pp.

Gives the best growth conditions for each type of plant.

Joint Liaison Committee on Plant Supplies (no date) *Plant list: trees, shrubs, conifers.* Reading: Horticultural Trades Association.

Keble Martin, W. (1986) *The concise British flora in colour.* 4th edn. by J. Taylor. London: Michael Joseph. 254pp. (ISBN 0718127005).

Glossary, detailed botanical descriptions and illustrations.

Maddison, Alan (1985) 'A modern approach to computerised plant selection (Computers in landscape practice)', *Landscape Design*, June, pp.37–8.

Program facilities, hardware and software for a landscape practice.

Philip, C. and Lord, T. (comps) (1987) *The plant finder.* Headmain for the Hardy Plant Society. 450pp. (ISBN 0951216104).

Lists over 22,000 plants available from some 300 nurseries.

Rice, G. (1988) *Plants for problem places.* Bromley, Kent: Christopher Helm.

Spencer-Jones, D. and Wade, M. (1986) *Aquatic plants: a guide to recognition.* ICI Professional products. 169pp. (ISBN 0901747033).

Spencer-Jones, D. and Wade, M. (1986) *Aquatic plants: a guide to recognition.* ICI Professional products. 169pp. (ISBN 0901747033).

Sturgess, P. (1985) 'Plant health and maintenance' *Landscape Design,* October, p.41.

Reports on the important growth in the understanding of plant health and maintenance.

Thomas, G.S. (1977) *Plants for ground cover.* Dent and Royal Horticultural Society. 282pp. (ISBN 0460039946).

Covers shrubs, climbing plants, conifers, herbaceous plants, grasses, rushes, ferns, annuals and biennials.

Planting

see also BS 3882, BS 5236

Austin, R.L. (1982) *Designing with plants.* London: Van Nostrand Reinhold. 190pp. (ISBN 0442246587).

Illustrations and diagrams accompany text on the ecology of planting design, analysis and implementation.

Beckett, K. and G. (1979) *Planting native trees and shrubs.* Jarrold. 64p.

Gives advice on what to plant and where to plant it, and how to raise trees and shrubs from seeds or cuttings.

Carpenter, P.L. and others (1975) *Plants in the landscape.* Oxford: W.H. Freeman. 481pp. (ISBN 0716707780).

An introduction to the principles and practices of ornamental horticulture in landscape architecture. Covers the history and development of landscape design and details of landscape contracting.

Clouston, B. (ed.) (1977) *Landscape design with plants.* London: Heinemann. 456pp. (ISBN 0434366501).

Includes designing with trees, forest planting, herbaceous plants and bulbs and also covers the technical aspects of planting in special conditions such as on spoiled land or in conditions of air pollution.

Cotton, S. (1988) *Guide to the specialist nurseries and garden suppliers in Britain and Ireland.* Woodbridge, Suffolk: Antique Collectors Club.

Hackett, B. (1979) *Planting design.* London: Spon. 174pp. (ISBN 0419127305).

Sets out the visual, ecological and economic principles of planting and provides a logical basis for the planting of particular trees, shrubs and other plants in different environments.

The planting and aftercare of trees and shrubs. (1979) Cheltenham, Glos.: Countryside Commission. Leaflet no. 3 (ISBN 0902590766).

Plants and Planting Methods for the Countryside. Perth: Countryside Commission for Scotland. Information Sheets.

A series of information sheets containing comprehensive advice on tree and shrub planting, on choice of species, and on the management of vegetation in some particular recreation areas such as beaches, and loch shores.

Pryce, S. (1988) 'Colourful and cheerful bedding displays', *Landscape Design*, February, pp.39–42.

Describes the variety of bedding plants now available and suggests ways in which landscape designers can use them to create colourful and interesting displays.

Roberts, D. and Bradshaw, A. (1986) 'Hydraulic seeding', *Landscape Design*, August, pp.42–7.

Hydroseeding can be a very economic and successful method of seeding steep slopes or inaccessible areas of topsoil, raw subsoil and derelict land material.

Thomas, G.S. (1984) *The art of planting.* Dent with National Trust. 323pp. (ISBN 0460046403).

Covers garden schemes (colour, styles of planting), plants, garden features and a list of plants for special purposes.

Play/Playgrounds

see also BS 5696

Baker, B. (1987) *Sports and play surfaces and associated equipment dictionary-directory.* Barry Baker Publications. 180pp.

An alphabetical list of terminology, products and firms relating to the construction of sports surfaces.

Heseltine, P. and Holborn, J. (1987) *Playgrounds: the planning, design and construction of play environments.* London: Mitchell Beazley. 204pp. (ISBN 0713452226).

Covers importance and development of playspace, playgrounds, installation, site design, planting and management.

Moore, R.C. (1986) *Childhood's domain, play and place in child development.* London: Croom Helm. 311pp. (ISBN 0856649368).

Explores children's habitats and looks at ways of conserving and creating childhood domains.

National Playing Fields Association (1987) *Impact absorbing surfaces.* London. 34pp. (ISBN 094608517X).

Describes the surfaces available and discusses their advantages and disadvantages, their ability to absorb the impact of a falling child and guidance on their installation.

National Playing Fields Association (1987) *Insurance for children's play*. London. 12pp. (ISBN 0946085145).

National Playing Fields Association (1988) *Playground equipment manufacturers list*. London. 7pp.

National Playing Fields Association (1987) *Playground management for local councils*. 2nd edn. London. 68pp. (ISBN 0946085161).

Looks at legal and insurance responsibilities and design considerations; inspection and maintenance procedures for playgrounds. Also includes an illustrated inspection guide to help identify common equipment faults.

National Playing Fields Association (1987) *Suppliers of impact absorbing surfaces for children's play areas*. London. 13pp.

Recreation

Equipment and Materials for Countryside Recreation Sites. Perth: Countryside Commission for Scotland. Information Sheets.

A series of information sheets available singly or in two ring binders, giving details on the construction, design and manufacturers of materials and products such as litter bins, gates, stiles, picnic furniture, etc., associated with recreation sites in the countryside.

Roads

see also BS 594, BS 1447, BS 4987, BS 5273

Crowe, S. (1960) *The landscape of roads*. Architectural Press. 136pp.

Emphasizes that road design and construction need qualified planners, architects and landscape architects and highway engineers in order to be absorbed naturally into the existing landscape pattern.

Department of the Environment (1977) *Parking in new housing schemes*. DOE Housing Development Notes VII (Parts 1 and 2). 24pp.

Covers levels of provision, planning and car space density and general requirements.

Department of the Environment (1977) *Residential roads and footpaths: Layout considerations*. London: HMSO. Design Bulletin no.32. 78pp. (ISBN 011750243X).

Considers effective provision for offstreet parking and pedestrian movement.

Department of Transport (1976) *Specification for road and bridge works*. 5th edn. London: HMSO. 194pp. O/P. (ISBN 0115503749). Supplement no. 1, 1978. 66pp. O/P. (ISBN 0115504753).

Design Council (1979) *Streets ahead*. 111pp. (ISBN 0850720818).

Stresses the mutual responsibility of planners, architects, businessmen, and shopkeepers in creating the street scene. Includes notes on the selection and siting of street furniture. Vandalism, signing systems, problems of cars in residential areas, advertising and shop front design come within the parameter of the book.

McCluskey, J. (1979) *Road form and townscape.* London: Architectural Press. 310pp. (ISBN 0851395481).

Covers the essentials of road engineering whilst bringing attention to the environmental context within which roads must be planned and built if they are to succeed with the people who have to use and live among them.

Shelterbelts

see also Fences and Walls

Ministry of Agriculture, Fisheries and Food (1977) *Shelterbelts for farmland.* London: HMSO. 27pp. (ISBN 0112406114).

Practical advice is given on the design, siting, establishment and maintenance of windbreaks with notes on the most suitable tree and shrub species for different conditions.

Ministry of Agriculture, Fisheries and Food (1979) *Windbreaks.* London. 39pp.

Provides practical details on windbreaks for a variety of purposes, eg for nursery stock, glasshouses. Advantages and disadvantages are discussed.

Patch, D. and Lines, R. (1981) *Winter shelter for agricultural stock.* Farnham, Surrey: Forestry Commission. 3pp. (Arboriculture Research Note 35/81/ SILN)

Signs

see also BS 873

Brown, A.C.H. (1974) *The construction and design of signs in the countryside.* Perth: Countryside Commission for Scotland. 41pp. (ISBN 0902226193).

The results of a study concerned with collecting, rationalizing and presenting information on the design of signs.

Street Furniture

Design Council (1979) *Street furniture.* Design Council. 192pp. (ISBN 0850720826).

A catalogue of products chosen by the Street Furniture Advisory Council for their high standard of design. Particular subjects covered are: street lighting; seating; planting; shelters and kiosks; and poster display units.

Gay, J. (1985) *Cast-iron: architecture and ornament, function and fantasy.* London: J. Murray. 112pp. (ISBN 0719542308).

A look at cast-iron as an element in architecture, verandahs, balconies, railings, gates, conservatories, decoration.

Littlewood, M. (1986) *Landscape detailing.* Architectural Press. 214pp. (ISBN 085139860X).

Comprises thirteen sections, ranging from free-standing walls to fences and gates, steps and ramps, drainage channels and tree surrounds. Each section begins with the technical guidance notes on design and specification followed by a set of drawn-to-scale sheets plus specification notes.

Thwaites, K. (1988) 'A reassessment of standards', *Landscape Design,* December, pp.15–17.

Calls for a revolution in the design and marketing of artefacts available for landscape work.

Warren, G. (1978) *Vanishing street furniture.* Newton Abbot: David & Charles. 159pp. (ISBN 0715374826).

Covers the development of such public utilities as street lighting, drinking fountains, water closets, milestones, etc., from earliest times to the Edwardian period, concentrating on the nineteenth century.

Timber

see also BS 881 and BS 589

Timber Research and Development Association (1985) *Preservative treatment for timber – a guide to specification.* High Wycombe: TRADA. 2pp.

Timber Research and Development Association (1987) *Timbers – their properties and uses.* High Wycombe: TRADA. 8pp.

The treatment of exterior timber against decay (1987) 2nd edn. Perth: Countryside Commission for Scotland. 24pp. (ISBN 0902226681).

Describes the causes and control of timber decay. It covers the role of preservatives, paints, varnishes, oils and exterior stain finishes.

Trees

see also BS 3936, BS 3998, BS 4043, BS 5236, BS 5837

Arboricultural Association (1983) *Trees in the 21st century.* Based on the First International Arboricultural Conference sponsored by the Arboricultural Association in conjunction with the International Association of Arboriculture. Berkhampsted, Herts: AB Academic Publishers. 133pp.

Papers on conservation policies to combat the destruction of large forests, the effect on landscapes of changing agricultural policies, urban development, disease and drought.

Arnold, H.F. (1980) *Trees in urban design.* New York/London: Van Nostrand Reinhold. 168pp. (ISBN 0442203365).

Advocates a fresh approach to the use of trees in urban environments. Design based on classical principles of grouping trees rather than scattering and is illustrated with regard to American cities. Individual species are assessed as to their suitability in landscape design.

Bean, W.J. (1970–1980) *Trees and shrubs hardy in the British Isles.* London: John Murray. vol. 1 A–C 8th edn. by G. Taylor, 1970 (ISBN 0719517907); vol. 2 D–M 8th edn. by G. Taylor, 1973 (ISBN 0719522560); vol. 3 N–Rh 8th edn. by D.L. Clarke and G. Taylor, 1976 (ISBN 071952427X); vol. 4 Ri–Z 8th edn. by D.L. Clarke and G. Taylor, 1980 (ISBN 0719524288).

Provides detailed descriptions.

Bean, W.J. (1988) *Trees and shrubs hardy in the British Isles.* Ed. D.L. Clarke. 8th rev. edn. Supplement to vols I–IV. London: John Murray. 616pp. (ISBN 0719544432).

Biddle, P.G. (1985) 'Arboricultural implications of revision of National House-Building Council: Practice Note 3 – Building near trees', *Arboricultural Journal,* vol. 9, no. 4, November, pp.243–9.

Discusses Practice Note 3 Root damage by trees; siting of dwellings and special precautions – published by the National House-Building Council Registration Council in 1969.

Bridgeman, P. (1979) *Trees for town and country: A practical guide to planting and care.* Newton Abbot: David and Charles. 144pp. (ISBN 0715378414).

Advises on the selection, planting and maintenance of the young tree, and lists the most suitable and attractive species for a variety of purposes and conditions. Other sections concern tree inspections, recognition of diseases, pruning, surgery and felling, with reference to the importance of trees on construction sites.

Browell, M. and Mead, H. (1987) 'Tree shelters', *Landscape Design,* April, pp.57–60.

Investigates the practical aspects of tree shelters designed to protect trees and shrubs from damage, to create a sheltered microclimate and to provide rapid establishment.

Clouston, B. and Stansfield, K. (eds.) (1981) *Trees in towns.* Architectural Press. 168pp. (ISBN 0851396585).

Discusses the importance of trees as visual elements in the townscape and provides advice on tree maintenance and care and repair of urban trees. Covers damage to foundations and drains caused by trees.

Davies, R.J. (1987) *Trees and weeds: weed control for successful tree establishment.* London: HMSO. Forestry Commission Handbook no. 2. 36pp. (ISBN 0117102083).

Looks at ways weeds can influence young trees and then discusses various methods of weed control.

Design guidelines trees: landscape design, planting and care (1985) London Borough of Richmond upon Thames. Leaflet.

Briefly describes enclosure, screen, planting, formal and informal planting, specimen planting, tree selection, site requirements, pruning and thinning.

Forestry Commission (1985) *Tree planting in colliery spoil.* By J. Jobling and R. Carnell. Edinburgh R&D Paper 136. (ISBN 0855381876).

Forestry Commission (1986) *Tree shelters: A guide to their use and information on suppliers.* prepared by Colin Shanks. Edinburgh. Spring. 7pp.

Offers advice on planting, weed control, stakes, erecting shelters, plastics and fastening methods, causes of failure and removal of shelters and ties.

Foster, R. (1982) *Trees and shrubs in garden design.* Newton Abbot: David and Charles. 231pp. (ISBN 0715382713).

Covers planting, care and cultivation, specimen trees and grouping of trees for maximum effect.

Gruffydd, D. *Tree form, size and colour: a guide to selection, planting and design.* London: Spon. 243pp. (ISBN 0419135200).

Includes guidance on design requirements, tree character, siting and display, light reflection, surface pattern, growth rate, atmospheric tolerance and planting distances.

Hillier, H.G. (1981) *Manual of trees and shrubs.* 5th rev. edn. Newton Abbot: David and Charles. 575pp. (ISBN 0715383027).

Provides descriptive and illustrative information on over 3500 woody plants.

Jaffa, G. (1984) 'Early recognition of tree disease', *Parks and Sports Grounds,* vol. 49, no. 7 April, pp.10–11.

Explains the difficulties in detecting disease in trees.

Littlewood, M. (1988) *Tree detailing.* London: Butterworth. 213pp. (ISBN 0408500026).

Covers stock, planting, pruning and surgery, protection of new trees and existing trees, tree surrounds, trees in containers, and roof gardens, maintenance and management, tree survey and evaluation.

Low, A.J. (1986) *Use of broadleaved species in upland forests – selection and establishment for environmental improvement.* London: HMSO. Forestry Commission Leaflet no. 88. 21pp.

Gives guidance on how best to select and establish broadleaved tree species for conservation, amenity and landscape purposes within upland coniferous forest areas of Great Britain.

Mitchell, A. and Jobling, J. (1984) *Decorative trees for country, town and garden.* London: HMSO. 146pp. (ISBN 0117100382).

Gives a visual aid to tree selection followed by sections on broadleaves and conifers. Details on features, merits, limitations, origins and cultivars are given for each species.

Mitchell, Alan (1985) 'Trees for towns and cities', *Arboricultural Journal*, November, pp.271–8.

Selection of trees for streets and restricted space.

Packham, R. and Bell, S. (1987) *Trees and the landowner.* Country Landowners Association. 30pp.

Looks at the law on preservation and felling of trees, forestry policy, procedure and grants.

Patch, D. (ed.) (1987) *Advances in practical arboriculture.* Proceedings of a seminar held at the University of York, 10–12 April 1985. London: HMSO Forestry Commission Bulletin no. 65. 196pp. (ISBN 0117102032).

Sections include: plant production; tree establishment; the mature tree and protection.

Patch, D. (1978) *Tree staking.* Farnham, Surrey: Arboriculture Advisory and Information Service. Arboriculture Research Note 40/87/ARB. 4pp.

Looks at reasons for and effects of staking. Also looks at minimizing the need for staking and treatment of previously staked trees.

Pepper, H.W., Rowe, J.J. and Tee, L.A. (1985) *Individual tree protection.* London: HMSO Forestry Commission Arboricultural Leaflet no. 10. 22pp.

Reviews the design requirements of individual tree protection and the ways in which these may be met in both the urban and rural environments.

Pepper, H.W. (1987) *Plastic mesh tree guards.* Farnham, Surrey: Arboriculture Advisory and Information Service Arboriculture Research Note 05/87/WILD. 9pp.

Describes light-degradable polyethylene plastic mesh tubes for use as tree guards to protect trees vulnerable to damage by rabbit or deer. Considers their use in towns.

Reader's Digest (1981) *Field guide to the trees and shrubs of Britain.* London. 303pp. (ISBN 0276002180).

Provides recognition profiles of more than 200 trees and shrubs, including all the species which grow wild in Britain and a wide selection of species introduced for garden and parkland planting.

Tabbish, P.M. (1986) *Rough handling reduces the viability of planting stock.* Farnham, Surrey: Forestry Commission Arboriculture Research Note 64/86/ SILN. 2pp.

Thoday, P.R. (ed.) (1983) *Tree establishment.* Proceedings of the symposium held at the University of Bath on 14–15 July 1983. University of Bath. 78pp.

Covers amenity sites, planting, transplanting, establishing trees on damaged soils and tree roots.

Thomas, G.S. (1983) *Trees in the landscape.* London: Jonathan Cape. 200pp. (ISBN 022402051X).

Concerned with the artistic use of trees in landscaping.

Turfs and Lawns

see also BS 3969

Joint Council for Landscape Industries (1980) *Rules for measurement for soft landscape works.* Joint Council for Landscape Industries and British Association of Landscape Industries. 23pp.

Provides rules of measurement for cultivating and preparing ground, grass seeding and turfing, planting, thinning and pruning, tree surgery, grass improvement and aftercare of growing material.

Hubbard, C.E. (1985) *Grasses: a guide to their structure, identification, uses and distribution in the British Isles.* 3rd edn. Harmondsworth: Penguin Books. 476pp. (ISBN 0140222790).

Pycraft, D. (1980) *Lawns, ground cover and weed control: creating and maintaining a lawn, alternatives to grass, using ground cover plants, controlling weeds.* London: Mitchell Beazley. 96pp. (ISBN 0855332190). (Royal Horticultural Society's Encyclopaedia of Practical Gardening).

Contains practical information and diagrams.

Shildrick, J.P. (1988) *Amenity pesticides '87.* Bingley, W. Yorks: National Turfgrass Council. Workshop Report no. 12.

York, P. (1988) 'Essential irrigation', *Landscape Design,* December, pp.48–9.

Introduces the aims and objectives of the British Turf Irrigation Association and stresses that irrigation should be considered right from the start of landscape design.

Urban Landscape

Cartwright, R.W. (1980) *The design of urban space: A GLC manual.* Greater London Council Architectural Press. 163pp. (ISBN 0851396933).

Provides practical guidance in the form of drawings, dimensional data, and comparative tables of costs on the equipping and furnishing of roads, pedestrian areas, cycle paths, subways, play areas, sign systems, lighting and other public facilities.

Cullen, G. (1971) *The concise townscape.* London: Architectural Press. 198pp. (ISBN 0851395686).

Illustrations show the jumble of buildings, streets and spaces which make up the urban environment and explore the visual effects which can be created.

Department of the Environment (1987) *Greening city sites: Good practice in urban regeneration.* London: HMSO. 127pp. (ISBN 0117520130).

Discusses individual projects on recreation, housing related improvements, visual enhancements, industrial and commercial areas.

Downing, M.F. (1977) *Landscape construction.* London: Spon. 247pp. (ISBN 0419108904).

Intended as an introduction to techniques and methods for the student landscape architect and covers such topics as site investigation, drainage and water features.

Dutton, R.A. and Bradshaw, A.D. *Land reclamation in cities.* London: HMSO. (ISBN 0117515604).

Explains ways in which grass, shrubs and trees can be established temporarily or permanently on urban wasteland.

Gage, M. and Vandenberg, M. (1975) *Hard landscape in concrete.* London: Architectural Press. (ISBN 0851392776).

Discusses the general problem of urban design with reference to the use of land surfaces in the formation of urban spaces. Covers the pedestrian and vehicle environment, street furniture and play areas. Information sheets give guidance on how to achieve desired finishes.

Steels, H.M. and Haigh, R. (1988) 'Looking at landfill', *Landscape Design,* December pp.50–4.

Describes how the 27 million tonnes of waste created in Cheshire is put to practical use by the local authority.

Tandy, C. (ed.) (1978) *Handbook of urban landscape.* London: Architectural Press. 275pp. (ISBN 0851396917).

Comprehensive coverage of the design procedure, surveys, plant data, parks, open spaces, recreation, gardens, housing estates, elements of landscape construction.

Taylor, L. (ed.) (1981) *Urban open spaces.* London: Academy Editions. 128pp.

Examines the importance of open spaces to the urban environment and how to protect and renew them. Applies to parks, plazas, playgrounds, streets, gardens, rooftops and waterfronts.

Walls

see also Fences, Hedges and Shelterbelts

Aldridge, T.M. (1986) *Boundaries, walls and fences.* London: Longman. 6th edn. 66pp. (ISBN 0851212344).

Brings together the various rules and laws relating to boundaries of private properties, as currently in force.

British Trust for Conservation Volunteers (1978) *Dry stone walling: A practical conservation handbook.* London. 120pp. (ISBN 0950164356).

Covers walls in the landscape, conservation of dry stone walls, law, safety equipment and organization, construction techniques and types of stone.

Garner, L. (1985) *Dry stone walls*. Aylesbury, Bucks: Shire Publications 32pp. (ISBN 0852636660).

Describes how to build, repair and maintain dry stone walls.

Korff, J.O.A. (1984) *Design of freestanding walls*. Brick Development Association. 35pp.

Guidance for civil and structural engineers, architects and builders to the design and use of plain and reinforced freestanding brick walls not forming part of a building.

Littlewood, M. (1984) *Landscape detailing*. Architectural Press. 152pp. (ISBN 0851398596).

Comprises 13 sections ranging from freestanding walls to fences and gates, steps and ramps, drainage channels and tree surrounds. Each section begins with technical guidance notes on design and specification (including a list of relevant British Standards).

Water in the Landscape

Campbell, C.S. (1978) *Water in landscape architecture*. London: Van Nostrand Reinhold. 128pp. (ISBN 1442214596).

Deals with the technicalities and aesthetics of fountain design. The art of design is put in an historical perspective. Outlines basic principles of hydraulics; practical limitations; environment; available equipment. A large section examines recent water features around the world.

Eachus Huckson Partnership and Shaw, F. (1988) *The water industry in the countryside*. Cheltenham, Glos.: Countryside Commission. CCP 239. (ISBN 0861701682).

Offers guidance on conservation principles, public access and recreation, general water treatment to water authorities and all others concerned and interested in water and the land.

Jellicoe, S. and Jellicoe, G. (1971) *Water: the use of water in landscape architecture*. Adam and Charles Black. 137pp. (ISBN 071361188X).

Extensively illustrated. Considers the nature of water; water in use; the philosophy of water; water landscapes of the past, present and future.

Robinette, G.O. (1984) *Water conservation in landscape design and management*. London: Van Nostrand Reinhold. 258pp. (ISBN 0442222041).

Covers all aspects of monitoring water usage, redesigning landscapes to use less water and applying water to plants in the most efficient way possible.

Travers Morgan (1987) *Changing river landscapes*. Cheltenham, Glos.: Countryside Commission. CCP 238. (ISBN 0861701615).

Assesses land use and landscape changes and their long term impact.

Wyson, A (1986) *Aquatecture: architecture and water*. London: Architectural Press. 216pp. (ISBN 0851397271).

Traces the history of the relationship between architecture and water, illustrates examples and gives practical advice on man-made landscape and water.

Woodlands

Crowther, R.E. and Evans, J. (1986) *Coppice*. 2nd edn. London: HMSO. Forestry Commission Leaflet no 83. 23pp.

Provides practical, managerial and silvicultural information for all those involved in coppice woodlands.

Evans, J. (1984) *Silviculture of broadleaved woodland*. London: HMSO. Forestry Commission Bulletin no 62. 232pp.

Describes silvicultural practices appropriate to a wide range of woodland types and conditions.

Managing small woodlands. (1980) Cheltenham, Glos.: Countryside Commission. Leaflet no. 6. (ISBN 0902590960).

Peterken, G.F. (1981) *Woodland conservation and management*. London: Chapman Hall. 328pp. (ISBN 0412128209).

Describes the origins, management and ecological characteristics of British woodlands. Shows how forestry and conservation can work in unison.

Small woods on farms. (1983) Cheltenham, Glos.: Countryside Commission. CCP 143. (ISBN 086170035X).

The Dartington Amenity Research Trust studied small woods in nine areas of England and Wales. Their report suggests ways of ensuring the future of these woods in the landscape, including management for timber as well as conservation and recreation.

British Standards

BS 187 : 1978 *Specification for calcium silicate (sandlime and flintlime) bricks*. Amendment no. 1 1987. BSI, 1978. 16pp.

BS 340 : 1979 *Specification for precast concrete kerbs, channels, edgings and quadrants*. BSI, 1979. 12.pp.

BS 497 : Part 1 : 1976 *Cast iron and cast steel*. BSI, 1976. 12pp.

BS 594 : Part 1 : 1985 *Hot-rolled asphalt for roads and other paved areas*. Part 1: Specification for constituent materials and asphalt mixtures. BSI, 1985. 15pp.

Specifies requirements for hot-rolled asphalt as laid as wearing course base course or roadbase for roads and over-paved areas. Includes guidance on selection of asphalt mixtures and their ingredients.

BS 873 : Part 6 : 1983 *Specification for retroreflective and non-retroreflective signs.* BSI, 1983. 12pp.

General constructional requirements for sign plates, frames and fittings, together with the photometric, colorimetric and performance requirements.

BS 873 : Part 1 : 1983 *Road traffic signs and internationally illuminated bollards.* Methods of test. BSI, 1983. 20pp.

Describes general test procedures for signs and bollards, including photometric tests, general strength tests and tests for assessing resistance to weathering and corrosion.

BS 873 : Part 3: 1980 *Specification for internally illuminated bollards.* BSI, 1980. 12pp.

Requirements for the design and performance of internally illuminated bollards excluding spring-back bollards.

BS 873 : Part 5 : 1983 *Specification for internally illuminated signs and external lighting luminaires.* BSI, 1983. 12pp.

General constructional requirements for signs incorporating a means of illumination, including requirements for electrical safety and light sources. Limits for the mean luminance and uniformity of luminance on the sign face are specified.

BS 881 and 589 : 1974 *Nomenclature of commercial timbers, including sources of supply.* BSI, 1974. 87pp.

BS 882 : 1983 *Specification for aggregates from natural sources for concrete.* Amendment no. 1, 1986. BSI, 1983. 12pp.

BS 1192 : Part 4 : 1984 *Recommendations for landscape drawings.* BSI, 1984. 40pp.

Includes symbols and abbreviations which are used in a series of typical drawings. Appendices include summaries of information commonly used when landscape drawings are being prepared.

BS 1147 : 1988 *Specification for mastic asphalt (limestone fine aggregate) for roads and footways.* BSI, 1988. 8pp.

BS 1722 : Part 2 : 1973 *Woven wire fences.* Amendment no. 1, 1976. BSI, 1973. 28pp.
BS 1722 : Part 3 : 1986 *Specification for strained wire fences.* BSI, 1986. 28pp.
BS 1722 : Part 4 : 1986 *Specification for cleft chestnut pale fences.* BSI, 1986. 12pp.
BS 1722 : Part 5 : 1986 *Specification for close boarded fences.*
BS 1722 : Part 6 : 1986 *Specification for wooden palisade fences.* BSI, 1986. 24pp.
BS 1722 : Part 7 : 1986 *Specification for wooden post and rail fences.* BSI, 1986. 16pp.
BS 1722 Part 8 : 1978 *Mild steel (low carbon steel) continuous bar fences.* BSI, 1978, 8pp.

BS 1722 : Part 9 : 1979 *Mild steel (low carbon steel) fences with round or square verticals and flat posts and horizontals.* BSI, 1979. 8pp.

BS 1722 : Part 11 : 1986 *Specification for woven wood and lap boarded panel fences.* BSI, 1986. 24pp.

BS 1722 : Part 12 : 1979 *Steel palisade fences.* BSI, 1979. 12pp.

BS 3882 : 1965 *Recommendations and classification for topsoil.* BSI, 1965. 9pp. Amd. 3089, no. 1, 1979.

Description of topsoil; classification by texture, pH., stone content. Notes on method of test for topsoil.

BS 3921 : 1985 *Specification for clay bricks.* BSI, 1985. 24pp.

BS 3936 : Part 1 : 1980 *Nursery stock: Specification for trees and shrubs.* BSI, 1980. 12pp.

Trees and shrubs, including conifers and woody climbing plants, suitable to be transplanted and grown for amenity. Covers origin, root system, condition, dimensions, packaging and labelling, and forms and sizes to be supplied for a wide range of species.

BS 3936 : Part 4 : 1984 *Specification for forest trees.* BSI, 1984. 8pp.

BS 3969 : 1965 (1978) *Recommendations for turf for general landscape purposes.* BSI, 1978. 8pp.

Provides details of desirable and undesirable grasses and weeds, soil, condition and dimensions of turves.

BS 3975 : Part 4 : 1966 *Plant description.* BSI, 1966. 28pp.

BS 3875 : Part 5 : 1969 *Horticultural, arboricultural and forestry practice.* BSI, 1969. 48pp.

Provides working definitions for terms commonly used in nursery practice, horticultural upkeep and ground maintenance, tree work and forestry.

BS 3998 : 1966 *Recommendations for tree work.* BSI, 1966. 32pp.

Covers safety and equipment; individual operations; cuts, pruning; lifting of crown; thinning; reducing; reshaping; restoration; repair work; bracing; feeding; tree removal.

BS 4043 : 1966 (1978) *Recommendations for transplanting semi-mature trees.* BSI, 1978. 28pp.

Comprehensive details on suitable trees for transplanting, season by season. Tree pits, drainage, tree lifting operations. Guying and securing the tree, wrapping, watering and spraying.

BS 4428 : 1969 (1979) *Recommendations for general landscape operations (excluding hard surfaces).* BSI, 1969 (1979). 52pp. Amd. 938, 1972.

Deals with the following general landscape operations: preparatory operations, including earthwork, land shaping and drainage; seeding of grass areas;

turfing; planting of shrubs, hedges, climbers, herbaceous plants and bulbs; individual tree planting, forestry planting for amenity purposes.

BS 4987 *Coated macadam for roads and other paved areas.* BS 4987 : Part 1 : 1988 *Specification for constituent materials and for mixtures.* 25pp.

BS 4987 : Part 2 : 1988 *Specification for transport, laying and compaction.* 8pp.

BS 5236 : 1975 *Recommendations for cultivation and planting of trees in the advanced nursery stock category.* BSI, 1975. 12pp.

BS 5273 : 1975 *Dense tar surfacing for roads and other paved areas.* BSI, 1975. 7pp.

Specifies the composition, manufacture, testing and transport of dense tar surfacing as defined in BS 892.

BS 5390: 1976 (1984) *Code of practice for stone masonry.* 44pp. Amendment no. 1, 1983.

BS 5628 : Part 3 : 1985 *Materials and components, design and workmanship.* Amendment no. 1, 1985. BSI, 1985. 104pp.

BS 5696 *Plant equipment intended for permanent installation outdoors.*
BS 5696 : Part 1 : 1986 *Methods of test.* 16pp. Amendment no. 1, 1987.
BS 5696 : Part 2 : 1986 *Specification for construction and performance.* 20pp.
BS 5696 : Part 3 : 1979 *Code of practice for installation and maintenance.* 8pp. Amendment no. 1 1980.

BS 5837 : 1980 *Code of practice for trees in relation to construction.* BSI, 1980. 28pp.

Principles to follow to achieve satisfactory juxtaposition of trees and construction. Recommends types of trees for planting near buildings, structures, plant and services. Advice on planting and maintenance of trees in urban locations and paved areas.

BS 6073 : Part 1 : 1981 *Specification for precast concrete masonry units.* Amendment no. 1, 1982. Amendment no. 2, 1984. BSI, 1981. 16pp.

BS 6431 : Part 22 : 1986 *Ceramic floor and wall tiles: method for determination of frost resistance.* BSI, 1986. 12pp.

BS 6677 *Clay and calcium silicate pavers for flexible pavements.*
BS 6677 : Part 1 : 1986 *Specification for pavers,* 12pp.
BS 6677 : Part 2 : 1986 *Code of practice for design of lightly trafficked pavements,* 12pp.
BS 6677 : Part 3 : 1986 *Method for construction of pavements,* 8pp.

BS 6717 : Part 1 : 1986 *Precast concrete paving blocks: specification for paving blocks.* BSI, 1986. 8pp.

INDEX

PICTURE INDEX

Photographic and illustration credits for the figures